A DALES HERITAGE

A Dales Heritage

Life stories from documents and folk memory

Marie Hartley and Joan Ingilby

First published in 1982

This new edition published in 1996 by
Smith Settle Ltd
Ilkley Road
Otley
West Yorkshire
LS21 3JP

ISBN   1 85825 040 4

British Library Cataloguing-in-Publication data:
A catalogue record for this book is available from the British Library.

Set in Montype Plantin.

Designed, printed and bound by
SMITH SETTLE
Ilkley Road, Otley, West Yorkshire LS21 3JP

Contents

Photographic Acknowledgements

Acknowledgements for use of photographs are as follows: Mrs M E Chapman, p13; from a print in Aysgarth Church, p32; North Yorkshire County Record Office, p49; Leeds Reference Library, p48; Mr H Metcalfe, p55; Mr J R Brown, pp71, 72, 79; Mr E Cooper, pp61, 90; Miss J Raw, p75; Stockton-on-Tees Green Dragon Yard art gallery, p88; Mr B Allen, p101; Mr and Mrs D Hall, p117; Mrs S Peacock, p118; Mr F Dinsdale, p125; Mr J Alderson, p147; Mr G Calvert, p155.

The rest of the photographs are taken from the Hartley/Ingilby collection of photographs, of which most were taken by Marie Hartley.

Introduction to the 1982 edition

The lives of comparatively few people emerge in sharp focus from the past, and in particular the detailed records of what we call ordinary people — artisans, craftsmen, farmers — are rare, especially if they are sought after in a specific area.

We have collected, during a lifetime's work, papers, account books, ledgers, wills, diaries, and in addition many memories of oral tradition, now unobtainable, which complement written material. From all these, by prolonged and patient scrutiny, we have pieced together the stories of a group of individuals who lived in the Yorkshire Dales from the mid-seventeenth to the twentieth centuries. In three cases, that of the yeomen farmers, the gamekeeper, and the blacksmith, we have had diaries and a day book lent to us.

The rest of the documents have come into our possession either as gifts or by purchase. For instance, the miller's ledger on which the work of George Terry, miller of Bainbridge mill in the late eighteenth century, is based, was sold at an auction sale of the goods of a descendant some 150 years later, and by good fortune we were there to bid for it. So much, alas, has gone in the periodic clearances of supposed rubbish in both household and business premises.

Each individual figuring in this book is typical of his or her time, but not one could be called famous or of national importance. All except three or four are of humble origin, excercising their traditional skills to make a living. Some showed greed, some altruism, some enterprise. A few fell on evil days not of their making. Such are the records which have survived that, although family relationships are evidently all-important, characters and aspirations only surface occasionally. Rather do their lives illumine the circumstances and the passage of events in the periods in which they lived. We also find a thread running through — a continuity of certain developments, such as the closing of the leadmines which affect many people and crop up in unlikely places.

Almost all were shaped by the same environment, that of the north country dales, which, especially in their upper reaches, experience a cold, wet climate with brief summers. Amongst the high fells there were and are few resources. Sometimes we wonder how so many people managed to exist where now their farmhouses and cottages lie abandoned by the former occupants. The weekender has often replaced large families who once swelled the numbers in village schools, and who day by day contributed to the continuity and enrichment of local life. Independence, self-reliance, neighbourliness and resilience were the characteristics of this breed of people, used to a simple existence in a bleak environment.

It was rare in upper dales villages to find a resident squire — a parson or nonconformist minister, yes, whose influence might be beneficial or negative. Education in the early days was minimal, until philanthropic men and women founded small schools, or dame schools catered for the young. Little money circulated, and grinding poverty followed only too rapidly on misfortune. Food was simple and housing crude by present-day standards.

These conditions, affected by the ups and downs of the economics of farming, industry and the weather, lasted from the seventeenth century to within living memory. The old society and the horse, which here vanished as motive power in the Second World War, more or less disappeared together. Perhaps the seventeenth century enjoyed the greatest prosperity before the population increased and too many people began to compete for too little work. Certainly, people in the nineteenth century endured extreme hardship as industry declined and drained away. Many forced to emigrate contributed sterling qualities to help found the new world.

Whether the old society was better or worse than that of the present day is arguable. Poverty has been ameliorated by the Welfare State and tourism brings prosperity to many, but no schemes were ever thought up in time, as they were in Norway and Sweden for example, to halt the draining away of the local population from the Dales.

Note to the new edition

Little revision has been necessary for the new edition of this book. It has been given a slightly different format, and the illustrations have been re-arranged. In the years since it was first published in 1982, a few old friends, whose recollections were valuable, have died. But mostly the book is concerned with the past, with farming and craftsmen, and often with leadmining and its impact on other people's lives from the seventeenth to the late nineteenth century.

MH & JI   1996

Families of Oxnop Gill

Oxnop Gill, a side valley descending into Swaledale a mile below Muker, is only three miles long. Two roads run down it — a narrow tarred road on the west side (Oxnop side) from Muker to Askrigg, and a rough track on the east from Satron (Satron side) also from Askrigg, both meeting at the summit of the pass by the Big Scar. In its small compass is to be found most of the ingredients of Dales life throughout the centuries — prehistory, monastic to present-day farming, a lost industry and depopulation.

Eight farmhouses are spaced about it: Hill Top, Gill Head and Heugh on the east side, and Oxnop Gill, two High Oxnops a field's length apart, Low Oxnop and Crow Trees on the west. Four of these are occupied as farmhouses: Oxnop Gill, Heugh, Crow Trees and Low Oxnop. Of the other four, the two High Oxnops are derelict and two are country cottages. Up to the first half of the last century, there were four dwellings and a cottage at Low Oxnop, a number long diminished to one farmhouse.

For at least two centuries, leadmining dominated Oxnop's story. Between the two roads, hardly an acre of ground has been spared the ravages of mining. Hushes — valleys deepened by artificial flooding — have torn and run-in shafts which pockmarked the hillsides with gullies and craters. All are healed over now by grass bitten close by sheep and in places prinked out in early summer with mountain pansies.

Even a smelt mill sited on Fors Beck once smelted ore from the rich Spout Gill leadmines below Hill Top Farm and other mines round about. A smithy once functioned on a level plot of ground at the head of the pass, and there was both an inn at Jenkin Gate and a beer house with a little garden below Hill Top. Miners' 'trods' or tracks led from stile to stile across the fields. Another relic is a water course, which can still be seen and traced, running for two miles from the top of Fors Beck on the west side of Oxnop round the head and on to a dam near Spout Gill on the east. It was a feat when in 1813 it was cut by leadminers in their spare time for a promise of £10.

Leadmining continued to the end. It is remembered that James Alderson of Gill Head in his early years worked at Old Gang, and before entering the mine he and his partners always stopped and said a prayer. As late as the First World War old

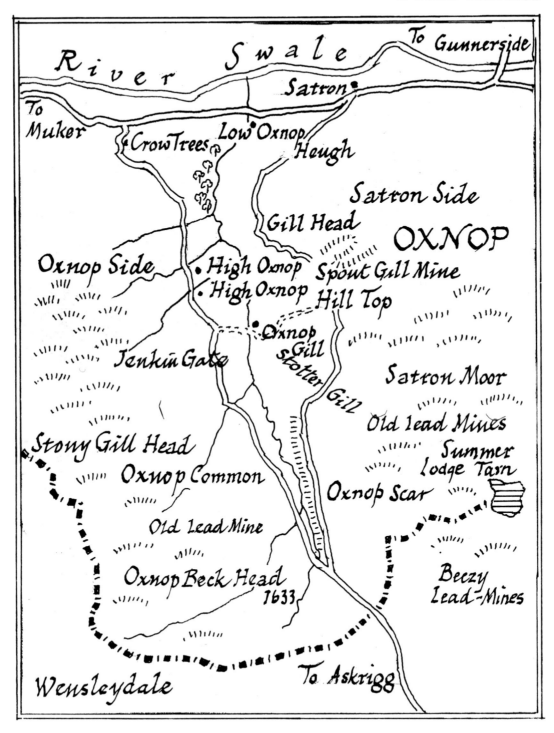

Looking down the Oxnop valley. Hill Top is on the right, and on the extreme left can be seen the chimneys of Oxnop Gill farmhouse.

Dodie Calvert from Satron worked alone in shafts at the head of the gill. The Guys of Hill Top gave him his dinner and carted his lead away, although it fetched no more than £12 a fother. Dodie ended his days alone except for the company of ten or twelve cats. Even in the 1920s a partnership was engaged in some leadmining in Stottergill behind Hill Top and elsewhere. The peace and quiet of Oxnop today belie the one-time industrial scene — the noise and smoke, the delving and the traffic.

Compared with the other ingredients in the gill's history, leadmining is comparatively modern. On Oxnop Gill Farm, under Castle Howe Scar, seemingly broken-down sheep folds are in reality the remains of hut dwellings of the Iron Age people, and flints have been found there. On this farm, too, a meadow is called Cow Sett, speaking of the Norsemen who established their *seters* in such places. For three centuries until the Dissolution, Oxnop formed part of the possessions of Rievaulx Abbey in upper Swaledale, and the monks had five tenants there called by still familiar names: Coates, Milner, Broderick and two Metcalfes.[1] Oxnop Gill, sited in a deep hollow by the waters of the gill, is an abbey site in miniature. A massive chimney remains from an earlier house, and the seventeenth-century doorhead with the initials and date SWR 1688 has been utilised as a lintel for an outbuilding.

Was it hereabouts that one night in 1605 a furtive figure, perhaps accompanied by a dog, lurked in the shadows of the gill? The figure stealthily rounded up first one sheep, then two or three, until six were being driven back over the fell top in the direction of Wensleydale. The thief, John Richardson, butcher, of Burton in Bishopdale, was caught and brought up at the North Riding Quarter Sessions at Richmond 'for stealing in Swawdale at a place called Oxenhopfell four sheep called sheep-hoggs, value 20s., and two ewes, value 12s., the property of George Wawne of Oxenhop.'[2]

More than 200 years later, in the early evening of Ash Wednesday, 1873, a boy was to be seen making his way down to Oxnop Gill farmhouse. That day he had visited Keld and Crackpot Hall carrying yarn for knitting, drapery goods and taking orders. The son of Thomas Gill, woollen manufacturer of Low Mill, Askrigg, William had been a half-timer working half a day at the mill and half a day at school, but now aged fourteen he was old enough to travel the round of his father's customers.

All day he had had but one thought. Ash Wednesday marked an event in the village Nonconformist calendar, the annual tea party at Bowbridge chapel between Askrigg and Bainbridge. He longed to be back in time for this, and hurrying along he had refused offers of meals which might have delayed him. But reaching Jenkin Gate he felt too weak to continue. He hitched up his pack, retraced his steps and turned down the track to Oxnop Gill where he knew that Peggy Kilburn, one of his father's customers, would give him food. Crossing over the beck on a slab of limestone to the house, he knocked at the door.

A woman in her forties opened it, and hearing of his plight asked him in.

'Thoo's varra sensible. What would ta like?'

'Weall, if ah mun 'a mi choice, some breead an' cheese an' milk.'

Soon a cloth was spread on a corner of the table pulled close to a hot peat fire, and the bread and cheese together with an apple tart laid on it. Peggy invited him to 'Reach to'. The house was quiet. Peggy's husband, George, and the farm man were out. George's old mother sat by the fire, and Peggy said she had work to do. When she returned, William had fallen asleep. The grandfather clock striking nine woke him.

'Nay', he said, 'Whyivver didn't ta waken me?'

'Weeal lad', she replied, 'Tha's had a good rest an' can buckle t' moor now.'

So he set out with a brisk tread to cross the fell top. But he was too late. As he hastened down to Askrigg, he met groups of people coming away from the Bowbridge tea party.

'Aye', said old William Gill, as he recounted this adventure seventy years later (he lived to be ninety-one and died in 1950), 'Ah were done tiv a set o' pins.' He went on, 'A neighbour o' mine used to tell me that she remembered seeing pass through

Low Row in Swaledale t' maister, servant girl and servant man from Oxnop Gill, all on horseback on t' way to Grinton church ter git wed. T' maister were George Kilburn and his bride, Peggy, was t' one 'at gev me t' food.'[3]

His neighbour had remembered the episode because her sister had been summoned to the farm to look after George's mother, then aged eighty-four, whilst they were away. Peggy was formerly Margaret Alderson of Rash, the servant man, John Kearton of Oxnop Gill and the servant girl, Jane Hall of Muker. Both couples were married on the 21st November 1868.

What William Gill didn't tell us — perhaps it seemed too painful a story — was that on the night of the 23rd March 1887 Peggy answered another knock on the door. She found a messenger come to break the news that soon after ten-thirty her husband, George, had been thrown from his horse and had fallen over the parapet of Muker Bridge on to the *carl* (stones) and had been killed instantly. He had had too good a night out. He was only sixty.[4]

The Kilburns had no children of their own, and had brought up a boy, William (Bill) Lambert, who then took over the farm. Bill o' t' Gill or Yoicks as he was known was noted for his strength, and used to carry huge burdens of hay to fodder his sheep in a pasture called Harricks which went with the farm and was well over the fell top in Wensleydale. He milked his cows out of doors in the 'Car Faud' (Cow Fold) and had a habit of wearing his shirt-tail outside his trousers in hot weather. In haytime his neighbour at Hill Top, Bob Guy, used to say, 'Bill has his butter clout out, we'll start mowing'.

Yoicks, too, liked a drink and sometimes rode over to one of the Askrigg inns and relied on his horse to carry him home. On the other hand, on Sunday nights it was his custom to take the steep winding track from Oxnop Gill to the Guys at Hill Top to smoke a pipe with them.

All the farmhouses in the gill have their own story to tell of the continuing cycle of life and death and the struggle for existence. Oxnop Gill, Low Oxnop and Crow Trees are the oldest buildings, dating from the seventeenth century, and Low Oxnop, sometimes called Oxnop Hall, is the least altered and exhibits interesting architectural features — decorative dripstones, a dated doorhead inscribed IEA (John and Elizabeth Alderson) 1685, an arched stone fireplace and massive beams. Here a dated doorhead, GKM 1739, from one of the old dwellings has been built into a barn. This now-demolished house was evidently the home of George Kearton, an eighteenth-century character who is said to have lived to be 125, and who died in 1764.[5] Another Kearton of Oxnop, Anthony, was in 1742 appointed gamekeeper to Thomas Smith, the lord of the manors of Healaugh and Muker. We shall meet both Keartons and Thomas Smith later on in this book.

In 1832, Lister Washington Metcalfe (1778—1846) bought the Low Oxnop property for £3,350. He was the son of the Rev Lister Metcalfe, for twenty-four years vicar of Muker, and he made a fortune as a merchant in Liverpool, as the large tombstones in Muker churchyard testify. A plaque above the dated doorhead on the porch at Low Oxnop records the initials of two of his four sons, James Simm and Booth Hay, and the date 1876. James Simm Metcalfe retired from farming and held a sale here in January 1869. The sale bill announced: 'Luncheon on the table at 11a.m. and the Sale to commence as near 12 o'clock as possible on account of the shortness of the Days.'[6]

He sold 'Six very superior roaned cows', four yearling stirks (young cattle), two calves, a bay cob filly, two fat pigs, and three superior Scotch tups. His tackle, then the full complement of a Dales farm, included two coup carts, two sets of cart gears, hemp and iron traces, backbands, two hay sledges, rakes, forks, two greasing stools (for salving), sheep cribs, salve kits, also dairy utensils — a barrel and a tub churn, three lead bowls, cans, cream pots, *siles* (sieves), bowls, butter scales and weights — and about 700 fleeces of 'Prime Scotch' wool. (His flock of *heughed* sheep would be left on the farm.)

In 1851 the four houses and the cottage at Low Oxnop were occupied by two families of Metcalfes, farmers, two families of Whitells, leadminers, and the cottage by an old woman, Mary Calvert, who had been a knitter and was now a pauper (an only too common a condition for the single and elderly). Twenty-one people in all lived there — fifteen over twenty-one and six under.[7] (Now there are two grown-ups and four children in one house.)

By 1871 all the houses and the cottage had been abandoned, and one farmhouse was occupied by Nancy Whitell, widow, with her four sons farming 275 acres, a

Low Oxnop Farm, showing the outbuildings converted and rebuilt from former houses.

William Gill in old age (c1940).

result of the amalgamation of holdings. Her third son, John (1846—1928), eventually took over the farm and bought it in 1925. John had five daughters and three sons, and at one time five of them were going to Muker School (closed in 1979). A farm man and a servant girl added to the household.

The children used to play in the old houses, known as old house, hen house, stable and sitting-room. A favourite game was playing at sheep farming with small fir cones for sheep and bits of stone for walls for pens. At Christmas the Pace Egg players came round, and Muker Aud Roy, a customary fair, still functioned but had dwindled to two stalls, one for sweets and the other for the butcher from Askrigg. For shopping they walked over the moor and took the train to Hawes. They had a trap, but would have had to walk up the steep pass anyway. Drinking water, usually two buckets a day, had to be fetched from a spring across the beck, and other water was provided from a huge 400 gallon rainwater tank and the beck. Nevertheless this was a cheese- and butter-making farm. They milked twelve dairy shorthorns of good quality — the cream always held a penny — and they made two tons of cheese in a season besides 70 lb of butter a week in the spring.

Jobs were apportioned. Mrs Whitell was generally the cheesemaker. She used a brass cheese-kettle in which were mixed the morning's and evening's milk. It was easier to make large cheeses so a few weighed 4 to 5 lb, but most were up to 17 lb each. Two or three big ones were made every day, pickled in brine, then dried. Most were sold wholesale by the hundredweight, averaging 6½d to 6¾d a pound. Odd ones might be sold privately at 7d a pound. Cheese to ripen and go blue was usually made in June and July, and one special pasture, Hazel Hill, had the reputation for grazing for the cows to produce blue cheese. Simon Moore's grocer's shop at Hawes was the outlet for the cheese. Moore sent round a traveller every eight weeks who sorted them out, then John Whitell took a load to Hawes by horse and cart. Moore sold many to a shop called Braithwaites at Stockton-on-Tees. Very little cheese was made in winter.

Buttermaking was allotted to Mary, one of the daughters. She used two churns, a barrel and a stand churn. The latter with its up and down plunger action was the harder work and was used for small quantities. Formerly they made round pounds stamped with the butter print of a thistle and leaves, but latterly they made long pounds. It was all that the maker could do after churning to clash, salt, weigh and print 30 lb of butter in an hour. It was sold at Muker to Tommy Guy from whom they obtained meal, flour and *proggin* (feeding cake for cattle).

The Whitells bought one of the first mowing machines in the dale, and when they tried it out in a meadow by the roadside, crowds of people came to see it. Joseph Whitell, farmer at High Oxnop, using an even earlier machine, asked if the blades couldn't be lowered an inch or so so as to cut more grass. In those days of the latter part of the nineteenth century they hired three Irishmen, brothers, who had come for years and who slept in the lofts of the old houses. Their wage was £6 a month and, if haytime spun on longer, £1 a week. The farm supplied the scythes but each man kept to his own. Sometimes they took an hour off for sharpening them on a grindstone. Strickles were for use when mowing. The oldest brother, Isaac, led them across a field in echelon formation, one a little behind the other, and all struck in unison.

John Whitell was 'very particular' to have the hay dry. It was put in footcocks two or three times and shaken out by hand because that way it parted and broke up better. Everyone had their own jobs. Isaac was the forker (forking the hay up through the forking-hole into the mew of the barn); another trod down the hay in the mew, and the third loaded sledges. Havercake, involving the baking beforehand of about forty of the large round cakes, was a standby. At the end they celebrated with a mell supper — meat and cake — which suited the Irishmen.[8]

All the eight Whitell children, except Hannah who died when she was twenty-one, married mostly into farming families. Hannah had been musical and joined with others in the valley in home concerts. Another, John the eldest son, took over the farm from his father and married Hannah Rutter. In turn their daughter and her husband, G B Porter, came to live there, and now the Porters' son and daughter-in-law and their four children live there.

Neither of the two High Oxnop farmhouses are now occupied. In 1851, Joseph Whitell with his wife and seven children lived in the top one. Joseph farmed ninety acres and employed two labourers. The lower one has been joined up to Low Oxnop, and on a June day in 1965 we attended the Porters' sheep clipping at the old unoccupied house. The sheep, 290 of them, were gathered in the paddock alongside and a professional clipper soon had them despatched — nineteen in the first hour, twenty in the second and twenty-one in the third. Soon we sat down round a table kept in the old kitchen for 10 o'clocks: bread, butter, scones, cheese, oatcake and ginger cake, with tea mashed with the spring water there noted for making a specially good brew. We went upstairs to look at a novel feature, an upstairs 'necessary' backing on to an outside wall with a chute like that in a castle. The kitchen and the rooms were cosy. It must have been nice living there.

Crow Trees, at the bottom of the pass on Oxnop side where the road plunges round bends into Swaledale, is one of the larger farms occupied now and for many years by the Hunters. We shall hear of this farm and its feasts in the chapter 'Base Metal'.

Relaxation was often found in music. At Gill Head in the nineteenth century James Alderson played the harmonium and another member of the family the clarionet, sometimes joining up with Hannah to play hymns.

The highest of the farmhouses in the gill, Hill Top, situated at about 1,300 feet above sea level on a plateau before the Satron road rises to the summit of the pass, is the newest house in the gill. It was built by John Clarkson (1780—1859) of Satron in 1834 to replace an older house, now a cowhouse below on the west. From the old house a dated doorhead inscribed IH 1721 has been inserted into the back wall of the new house. Here the Clarksons lived for a short time with their two young daughters, Barbara and Mary, a governess, and one female and two men servants.[9] (Barbara, who died in 1914, is remembered because she grew up to be enormously fat and for transport had to use a farm cart.) At the front of the large well-built house is a paved path, cobbles, a low wall protecting a garden, and, in an alcove in the high west wall, two massive stone cheese presses.

A narrow ancient road, that which Yoicks climbed every Sunday, winds down from Hill Top past the old house to Oxnop Gill farmhouse and so to the west road on Oxnop side, a route followed by horse and trap to Muker from Hill Top until the motor car era. It is tempting to think of it as a connecting track between the properties of the monks of Rievaulx in the Middle Ages.

Hill Top became a farm for young people starting up, hence tenants moved in and out frequently. In 1846 Thomas Whitfield paid £65 a year rent for the farm. In 1854 he was followed by Thomas Whitton who had twenty-five acres of meadow, fifty-six acres of pasture land, unlimited right of common in the manors of Healaugh and Muker, also ninety-four ewes and twenty-nine gimmer hogs (young female sheep) which went with the farm (*heughed* sheep as was the common practice). But three years later Thomas left and the new tenant, Edward Boland, paid £95 a year for rent. The next one, Thomas Waggett, had his rent raised in 1865 to £98.[10]

Finally came three generations of Guys, tenants of the Clarksons for nearly 100 years. About 1875 Richard and Rosamund Guy, with their three sons and a daughter, moved from Skeugh Head near Angram, upper Swaledale, to Hill Top. Richard was interested in astronomy and passed on his hobby to his sons. He and two brothers performed as some of the music men in Muker Church where Richard played the bass fiddle.

One Sunday, 30th July 1882, on his way to church he detoured to take a look at a bull which he had brought up. The bull, apparently not recognising him in his Sunday clothes, gored and killed him. He was in the prime of life, forty-nine. The widow and the three sons carried on, one starting a meal, butter and eggs business, which later continued at Muker as a provision merchant's. Eventually one of them, Robert John (1863—1936), took over the farm himself. (By now the top High Oxnop Farm, Joseph Whitell's, had been joined to Hill Top so that it was a larger unit.) It happened to be the severe winter of 1895 and Bob went nine weeks without speaking to anyone. He lived on bacon, potatoes and eggs. He had hay and cake for the cows which were dry as was usual in winter, and he fed the sheep on Indian corn which was strewn on the hard, frozen snow.

In September of that year, partly not wishing to face another winter alone, Bob married Isabella Hunter, and here they brought up four children, two boys and two girls. At the start, the young couple decided that they had to be very careful. When at the end of the month the grocery bill came in, they looked at it and shook their

Hill Top Farm in haytime during the 1950s. The barn to the right of the trees is on the site of an older house. Spout Gill is in the foreground.

heads. It amounted to a guinea, not much because they had their own butter, cheese and lard. Isabella went down it, and came to the conclusion that the only item they could do without was Bob's tobacco, so she crossed it out. After that he always had to buy his own.

The Clarksons, the landlords, lived at Satron, and Mary, not the stout sister who was the dominant one, nevertheless kept a sharp eye on the farm. If a stone was down from a wall, she would point it out, or send word that there were some *mowdies* (moles) which needed catching. In any case the farm was very well kept. If they were in pocket at the end of the year, if it were no more than £10 and if the stock had increased, well and good. They were happy.

In those days, at the turn of the century, Bob kept all his money in gold sovereigns in a locked drawer in a chest of drawers in a bedroom. The children were allowed to dip their fingers in to touch the sovereigns and half sovereigns. Then, a representative of a bank came to Muker and explained about starting a bank account and writing on bits of paper. Bob listened and went back to discuss it with Isabella, but it was a long time before they came to a decision. In the end Bob took

600 gold sovereigns in a bag, swinging it in his hand, to Hawes. After that they used to say that they never had any money again.

Isabella worked hard on the farm, and always had beautiful hands from handling the sheep, milking and making cheese. For this, too, was a cheesemaking farm. They milked fourteen cows and made three or four cheeses a day, so that they needed the two huge presses which were in regular use up to about 1925. If anyone came to visit, Isabella didn't take them into the parlour or dining-room but straight up into the cheese room. This was her great interest. The shelves were regularly washed down, and if the calico bandages became dirtied with the constant turning she always put on new ones.

From about 1905 to 1921 (before that he went to Yarm Fair) Bob Guy, starting at 3.30am on a sixteen-mile journey, took twenty or thirty cheeses and ten heavier ones by horse and cart across Swaledale and Arkengarthdale and over the Stang to Barnard Castle. Here he stood the market once a fortnight on a Wednesday. Mostly his customers were miners. Occasionally if times were bad he went as far as Middleton-in-Teesdale. Paid in gold sovereigns, he brought them back in his pocket and slid them out into the drawer.

The two girls, Maggie and Mary, undertook the housework which included washing and sanding the floors about every three days. Lumps of sandstone were collected from a gill and beaten down into fine sand. Saturday was specially busy, and usually work wasn't finished until after tea, and in haytime it might be 11pm and later. On that day the sand had to be swept up from the floor of the forehouse and other rooms except the parlour. Then the floors were scrubbed and fresh sand put down. 'It looked lovely.'

After sanding was given up, Isabella wiped the floor with whey which gave it a polish. The firestone was washed with a drop of milk in the water so that the decorations drawn with a limestone stick stuck and did not easily rub off. All the furniture had to be polished. Then the bath tub was brought out and the children bathed. Then father had his bath and shaved even if it was 11pm so as not to encroach on Sunday. It was customary for farmers then to shave once a week.

Bob was good at figures but not much of a reader. Now, on Saturday night when all the family was ready, the children sat up to hear their mother read the *Darlington and Stockton Times*. Beginning with births, marriages and deaths, she read right through to the farm stock reports. The children loved it. After that Bob always carried them piggy-back upstairs in turn.

The children walked, and after Mary was born, rode the two and a half miles to Muker School, taking sandwiches and leaving the pony in an uncle's stable. Once an old woman asked Maggie to go and get her a clay pipe for which she gave her a penny. To her dismay she dropped and broke the pipe, but her grandmother saved the day by giving her a penny to buy another.

On Sundays the children going to Sunday school walked twice that day to Muker,

The Guys' wedding group in 1895. From left to right: John Peacock, Robert John Guy, Isabella Hunter, John Scott, Robert Brown. Seated: Elizabeth Raw, Elizabeth Guy, Elizabeth Whitfield.

whilst their parents went to their respective places of worship — one was church and the other chapel. The better-off farmers' wives there usually made a boiling of beef and bacon in a huge pan on the fire that day, and Maggie as a child took jugfuls to poor people who looked forward to it. Sabbath observances at Hill Top were strict. The reading of newspapers or books was forbidden, and even the gathering of rhubarb from the garden was regarded as work. Rabbit was a favourite dish and the children had to clean up all the bones on their plates. Bread and butter or bread and jam, never all three, was the rule.

The children used to go to Gunnerside to have their clogs repaired. Irons were put on whilst they waited. On the way back they often called on the Clarkson sisters at Satron. They thought that Maggie ought to learn to dance, and the housekeeper taught her to the tunes of a wind-up box-organ. Then, she was ready to go to her first dance at Muker.

Crow Trees, Oxnop, Swaledale, c1935. The house, extended since the seventeenth century, has developed from a long house. The trees have since gone.

The two girls married, and in 1932 Jack Guy followed his father as tenant at Hill Top where his wife continued to make cheese until about 1950. They retired from the farm in the early 1970s. It was sold by a descendant of the old Clarksons, and now the land is let off and newcomers have bought the house as a second home.

Maggie and her sister, Mary, both agree that there is nothing like being a farmer's wife. They loved the work. Maggie clipped fifty sheep when she was seventy, and declared that 'she would do it all ovver again'.

1   *Cartularium Rievellense*, Surtees Society, Vol LXXXIII (1889).
2   Quarter Session Records edited by J C Atkinson, *North Riding Record Society, Vol 1*, pp 13-14.
3   Recollections of William Gill, 1859-1950.
4   'Diary of John Dunn of Muker'. Notes from Fawcett MS.
5   Clarkson Account Book lent by Mr M Clarkson and NYCRO PR/MUK/1/8.
6   'Valuation of Oxnop Hamlet' (1856) and Sale Bill (1869) lent by Mrs H Whitell.
7   PRO Ho107/2380 Enumerated census.
8   Recollections of Mrs M Waggett, b 1887.
9   PRO Ho107/2380 enumerated census.
10   Clarkson Account Book.
11   Recollections of Mrs M E Chapman, b 1898.

Two Seventeenth-Century Leadmine Proprietors

LEADMINING IN THE COMMONWEALTH

The story of Arkengarthdale was dominated through almost three centuries by leadmining and relics of the industry, visible on the roadside and on the slopes of the hills, are more obvious here than elsewhere. In the early nineteenth century almost 1,500 people lived in the dale, a number reduced since mining ceased to a couple of hundred.

From the Middle Ages onwards, lead has been mined in the dale and leases taken from the Crown who owned it as part of the Lordships of Middleham and Richmond. But in the 1650s the new manorial lord, Dr John Bathurst, began in a modest way what was eventually to become extensive exploitation of the mineral wealth. His sons, John, Charles and Theodore, employing agents, carried on the mines, and either the initials of Theodore's son, Charles (1673—1724), or more likely his son, another Charles, who was High Sheriff of Yorkshire and MP for Richmond in 1727, were adopted for the famous CB mines.

Dr John Bathurst lived in Blackfriars, London, had five sons and three daughters, and one of his claims to fame was that he was physician to Oliver Cromwell. When in 1635 he married Elizabeth Willance, heiress of the manor of Clints in lower Swaledale, he entered the stage as a landowner in the north. In 1654, acting through an intermediary, Major Norton of St Nicholas near Richmond, he leased lead and coalmines in Arkengarthdale and the adjoining New Forest for twenty-one years from the citizens of London, paying £24 10s and a yearly rent of 6d.[1] (The citizens had had the Lordships conveyed to them by Charles I for the payment of debts.) Two years later, striking a bargain through Major Norton, Dr John bought the manor of Arkengarthdale and other property in Richmondshire for £2,100 from the citizens who reserved the mineral rights. The yearly value of Arkengarthdale then totalled £56 18s 6d.[2]

A shabby book of forty-six pages, backed with rough brown paper, records the accounts 'both of the leade works and other estates' of Dr John kept by his agent, Benjamin Purchas, also of St Nicholas. Covering a little over a year from the 1st August 1657, it reveals the beginning of the Bathursts' involvement in mining in the dale.[3]

*Arkengarthdale, with Arkle Town in the foreground and Langthwaite Church
in the centre distance.*

The doctor's five grouves or groves, as they were called, lay on both sides of the
dale, and were each worked from one or two shafts by partnerships of four (one
three) who were paid for the loads of ore won. About twenty miners, including a
widow, were thus employed, some working at more than one shaft.

The agent devotes about half a page to each mine, and makes comments in the
margins. The first shaft of the White Gang on Booze Moor, worked by John
Barningham, James Peacock, Widow Willies and William Murton, is 'a very good
and hopefull Shaft', but the second is 'amost wrought out'. The partners at the first
shaft, paid for at the rate of 19s a bing-load of ore at roughly monthly intervals, earn
in the year £214 5s 6d, and on the opposite page the amount of lead ore received
from them is recorded, 247½ loads.[4] The monthly payments fluctuate violently from
£9 10s in February to £49 8s and £45 2s 6d in November and December, obviously
a burst of activity before winter set in. No payments are usually made in January or
February, and at one mine none until May.

Of the second shaft of High Windegge, also on Booze Moor, we read: 'This Shaft quit, given over & Geo Scot run away but the other 3 partnars woorke at the Second Shaft of the White Gange.' At Mouldersit, west of Langcliffe, the 'Eastmist Shaft' worked by John Barningham, James Peacock, James Collinge, and Thomas Coates is 'the best & hopefullest Shaft & very rich gittings only hindred by water. Memo: upon this Vaine 2 Shafts more all ready sunke for tryall.' The rate for the trial was increased to £1 2s a load. One of Dr John's many directives reads: 'for the waytered worke let the workmen be incouraged by givinge sume small sumes, so often as B.P. shall judge fit.'

The accounts are complicated by the borrowing which prevailed. Almost every-one, including the smelters, was in debt. For instance, although the partners at the White Gang had raised 247½ loads of ore, they were only paid for 225½. The twenty-two loads deducted cancelled out previous debts, and 'Cleare' is now written at the bottom of their column of figures. A further list of individual miners record debts ranging from shillings to £2 8s 8d, and one of the smelters, Ralph Warde, owing £3, had paid off part leaving him still owing £1 15s. Dr John acted as local banker, not only lending money to his workmen but to members of the gentry by issuing bonds for sums ranging from £50 to over £300. Again comments are made. Some are 'good hopefull debts' but others are 'doubtful'.

The rate for the smelters was 10s 6d for smelting a fother and 2d a fother for weighing. Between them they received £39 16s 3d during the year. Ralphe Warde also chopped wood and the other smelter, John Taylor, built up 'Orgait house in Clints ground which was burnt' for £1 2s 6d.

At that date Clints Mill on the doctor's estate near Marske smelted the ore from

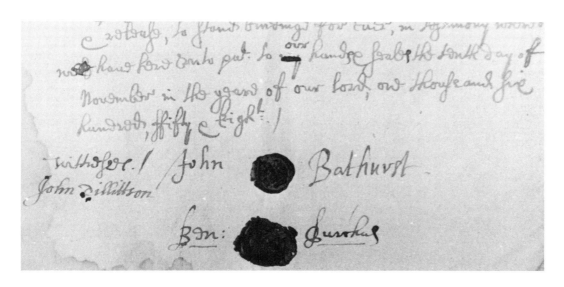

Dr John Bathurst's signature, 1658.

Arkengarthdale. An inventory taken of the work tools there reads: 'one paire of Bellowes well furnished, one Iron weigh backe with the weights weyeth 100¾ and 24 pounds, 7 old chop sacks, 4 new ones, about 25 oare pockes [bags], 5 gavelocks [crowbars], 35 new oare pockes, 8 old shovells, two buckars [for crushing ore], two picks, a new Iron mell [hammer], 3 marking hamars, one old leade pann, two ladles, one old axe, 4 new fiar shovells, two ore troughs.'

Carriage, in this case from Windegg to Clints, seven miles, was as always a heavy expense. William Milnar, the ore carrier, was paid at the rate of 2s 2d a load, and transporting 473½ loads of ore earned £56 19s, which included housing it, also a man leading flags and clay for the mill race and for leading sods for the kiln roof.

The collier's bill on the other hand is small, only 100 loads at 1s a load for the year. No mention is made of where the pits are, but Dr John again gives a directive 'for tryall for Coles let a man of judgement and experience maike tryall, at some convenient times, and if incouraged then consider how to proceed further in that.'

The wood leader's bill hints at relentless denudation. Thorn wood is taken from the Horse Close at Clints at 2d a sack, and whin wood from Bell's whin woods at Aske at 6d a sack, in all 679 sacks costing £14 9s 10d plus £7 17s paid to the owner of the wood. The wood-cutters, working in partnerships, chop it all up and are paid 4d, sometimes 6d a sack, adding up to £12 11s 2d. There is no mention of kilns for drying. Lastly comes the excise-master's bill, paid in eight instalments at the rate of 6s 8d a fother, in all £24 4s.

Besides these, two pages of 'Necessary Charges' add to the general picture. A selection reads:

pd to the Smyth of Maske for mendinge 4 gavelocks and for maikinge 60 nayles for the Use of the Miln [probably for the bellows]	00:06:02
pd for 22 yards of Sacke web for oare pockes with pack thred for maikinge them with [bags both for carrying the ore out of the mine and to the smelt mill]	00:16:06
pd the Smyth of Maske for maikinge a bucar [ore crusher] and some odd things for the Use of the Mill	00:02:00
pd for mending the oare house	00:02:00
pd a wright for mendinge the Miln Axletree and for an Iron houpe for the Axletree	00:11:06
pd for a tand hide for maikinge water baggs for clearinge the water at Windegge that they may worke	01:06:08
pd for 15 yards and 3 quarters of harden for maikinge chop [wood] sacks on	00:13:00
pd for a house building up in Arkingarthdayle for keepinge the cut wood safely their	02:00:00
pd for a doore, crookes, bands and a locke for it	00:02:00
for the carrage of the Grouvars tobaco from London	00:01:00
pd to the Smelters for 11 dayes worke at the mill raise and at the kill[n]	00:05:06
pd for Iron and maikinge up a great Hamar	00:04:06
pd for the carrage of one ore trough from Fremington to the Mill [a trough for washing]	00:00:06

pd in charges for 4 nights when oare was taiken up [a regular disbursement]	00:06:00
pd for a house that the lead laye in at Stockton [Stockton was the inland port for the despatch of lead by sea to London and abroad]	00:10:00
pd for 7 loades of stones for the Mill Harth	00:02:04
given to the Smelters and other men in ayle	00:01:00
The total including many other items	14: 16:00

Finally, during the year 1,400 pieces, that is 70 fother at 22 cwt, the Stockton fother, were sold at the rate of around £14 each to Francis Lascelles for £1,056 15s 11d. £767 2s 6d of this was paid to the doctor in London in three instalments sent by bills of exchange — one to Mr John Swale 'at the winde mill neare Billinsgaite'.

The book of accounts also includes rentals, miscellaneous disbursements and charities. When Dr John bought the manor, as already stated the yearly value was £56 18s 6d with small amounts of rents and fines reserved. Revision of rents was long overdue, but naturally when introduced immediately after the purchase they were resisted. Many rents, not all, were increased tenfold, plus a small fine on death or change of ownership and a renewal fine every twenty-one years. For example Bryan Peacock of Sealhouses had paid 10s 5d, increased to £5 3d plus 8s and 16s for the two fines. Some only paid shillings, and Cuthbert Hird of Eskeleth paid the most, £3 17s 1d old rent and £30 new. There were about forty tenants in Arkengarthdale. The doctor, losing his temper at their intransigence, threatened to send them to Barbary or Ireland. But he succeeded in making new contracts and raised his receipts to over £500 a year.[5]

One of his directives states: 'Retourne back to Bryan Hird at Martinmas next his halfe yeares rent: being 20s. as a token from the Dr.' In the 1660s his second son, John, who followed him as landlord, allowed his tenants a fifth of their rent 'in respect of hard times'.

Amongst the entries in the year's accounts are repairs to houses, locks (there must have been dishonest people about), the agent's salary (£20 for the first year and £30 for the second), seventeen steers to stock a pasture at Clints, parchment, wax (for seals for documents), a book for the manor courts, the buying of horses and expenses on journeys to London. Two entries read: 'pd for a Horse for John Place [the clerk] the old mayre beinge dead — £3' and 'for a Mayre for myselfe [B. Purchas] to ride on — left at London and a horse taiken away — £6. 6s. 8d.'

On other pages are particulars of the doctor's many charities paid for out of the revenue of the estates. He gave £8 a year for poor scholars for two exhibitions to Cambridge 'until they be Master of Arts', and an entry reads: 'rec. of Willm Collinge for money you were pleased to retourne to his sonn John to Cambridge — £3.' This charity was linked with the sum of £4 a year with which to bind an apprentice. (The former, now absorbed into other bequests, was administered by Richmond Grammar School, and the latter is still awarded.)[6]

He also founded three schools at New Forest, east of Arkengarthdale, Marske and in the dale itself for his tenants, almost all of whom were illiterate. A salary of £16 a year for a master for the dale school was proposed, 'desiringe them to looke out a fit man, and J.B. approving him'. Sums were paid to the poor in different places, and 1s a quarter to poor widows if they go to church. All in all, disbursements added up to £2,170 7s 6d, and receipts, chiefly the lead works and rents, to £2,162 16s 11d — a deficit over the year of £8 10s 7d due to the agent.

Dr John was member of parliament for Richmond in 1655 and 1658. Amongst his property his 'greate House' in Richmond was occupied by William Wetwange, a rich hosier and the first mayor of the town, and was on the site of the King's Head Hotel. From time to time he came to his manor house at Clints and intervened personally in estate problems. He combined a businesslike with a philanthropic approach proper to a Puritan, and in one way or another had an enormous impact on his tenants. Of one who was described as 'unworthy' he decreed: 'yet let him be used as others of his Condition, but agree not with him, but upon satisfactory reasons.' For another, Widow Collinge, he arranged for her two younger sons to have tenements at Booze and Arkle Town if it could be legally managed, and for her to have 20s a year. He ends this last order in 1658 with the words 'to testifye the truth of this in case of Mortallity this is the will of J.B.' He died the following year.

LEADMINING AT THE RESTORATION

A second manuscript book of fourteen leaves contains John Fawcett's accounts for the lead works of Thomas Swinburne at Hurst and at Copperthwaite above Fremington Edge in Swaledale from November 1660 to June 1663. Swinburne belonged to an important Catholic family, of whom Algernon Charles Swinburne, the Victorian poet, was an indirect descendant. He lived at Barmpton, near Darlington, and was in the 1660s lord of the manor of Marrick, where John, his son, occupied the manor house. His agent, John Fawcett, lived in the parish.[7]

The accounts are set out differently from those of Dr Bathurst. Individual miners are listed and far fewer have local names. In 1660 twenty-three of them, in 1661 seventeen, and in 1662 twenty, including two or three women, usually wives and daughters, earn from £63 to as little as 17s in the year. They are paid 17s, occasionally 18s, for a bing load of ore. (Both wages and the price of lead had dropped.)

About half the same men are also paid by fathom tale, that is for sinking shafts, mostly at 4s 6d a fathom (six feet), and less frequently for driving levels at 2s a fathom. In 1664, 427 fathoms were driven. Other payments include 'repairing and beating up the level' (beating is a method of carrying away the water) at 10d a fathom, and '3 pounds of Candles to work with in the Level' at 6½d a pound. Nor is there strict demarcation of jobs. Some of the grovers (miners) in partnerships of four draw dozens of timber at 8d a dozen.

Thomas Fawcett, John Tirry, old Raife and young Raife Loftus and others are the carriers. They lead horse loads of ore from Hurst and Copperthwaite (about twice as much from Hurst) to the High and Low Mills at Marrick, dozens of timber from adjoining estates, horse-loads of stoprice (for wood for the shafts), sacks of chopwood, 'Coles to Hurst to firewith in the Levill' (a method of softening the rock), and over 1,000 horse-loads of slags from old smeltings on Fremington Edge and Skelton Moor to the mills. Finally, pieces of lead at 6s 8d a fother were carried to Hartforth, the half-way house to Stockton, and occasionally a small amount, for instance six pieces at 20d a piece for carriage, were sent to Bishop Auckland for the Bishop of Durham. John Tirry also earned £3 14s 11d for smith work for two years at the High and Low Mills.

Similar disbursements to those of the mines in Arkengarthdale recur: yards of harden at 10d a yard for chop sacks and ore pokes, leather water-bags 'for drawing water with in the groves', and three boards 'for casting of[f] one when they worke in the grove'. Nor are the works free from dispute. Twice money was paid, once '18s. amongst the workmen when Mr. Hutton [John Hutton of Marske] came and distrained there ore and there grove ropes'; and again 4s 'at several times to the Smelters in drinke to in Courridge them when Mr Hutton came and distrained the lead and threateinge them for workinge for Mr Swinburne.'

At that time the High and Low Mills on Dale Beck north of Marrick and three miles from Hurst were important but ruinous. Both were in use, both had chimneys and slag hearths, and they were connected by a goit for water for the water wheels which worked the bellows which created the draught on the hearths. Dams nearby fed a water race connected to the goits. Lead from other mines was smelted there, and the High, although requiring more repairs, smelted six times more than the Low.

In August 1661 the High Mill was partly re-slated and sods laid on the roof after storm damage. The building was pointed all over, and the chimney plastered with hair plaster. Three hundred 'tackits' (broadheaded nails), costing 9d, and half a hide of leather were bought to mend the bellows, which also needed three quarts of oil and half a stone of tallow mixed together for 'lickering' (smearing on to keep the leather supple), plus half a peck of meal for the bellows, perhaps to remove rust on iron parts. Gudgeons (sockets) were repaired and replaced. The kilhole (kiln-hole part of the furnace), walls and doors were mended, and six kilbaucks (beams) were felled, led to the mill at 8d a kilbauck, and placed in position.

The Low Mill required '148 harths of stones', a new sump (the cast iron pot let into the floor into which the molten lead ran), and Francis Greathead was paid 17s 'for supplying it, liinge it in and mendeinge the low mill flowre'. Its bellows and chimney needed some attention too.

'Coles' were led for the High mill at 20d a quarter, and a coal hole housed fuel from Colepit Moor where it had been burnt for cinders. Coopers repaired tubs;

Marrick High Mill.

others mended dams, and Thomas Hudson sawed two thorn trees, specially bought, into taps and tridles (treadles), mended the Low Mill bellows, the chimney and 'putinge tridles and taps'. Scuttles for carrying ore, riddles, iron ones to riddle slags, stones to mend the kiln-holes, hundreds of kilrods, chopwood and lead ore were led by the eight carriers, who earned sums ranging from £20 to £74. Lastly, the amount of lead smelted, receipts and expenses for the three years are summed up — 201 fothers and nine pieces of lead were smelted at 7s a fother at the High Mill, and thirty-six fothers and sixteen pieces at 22s a fother at the Low, which, plus dressing ashes, blackwork (slag), serving the hearths and some repairs, cost £269 17s 1d.

Most of the lead was sold to Mr Peers of Stockton at £10 a fother and made £2,353 9s 7½d, plus £113 1s for smelting other people's ore at £2 2s a fother, plus rents at Marrick, in all £2,559 9s 7½d. Alas, £2,678 10s 1½d was paid out, leaving a loss of £119 0s 6d still to disburse. 'As a note will make appeare', wrote John Fawcett.

The result was discouraging. By 1668, when Thomas Swinburne had died, his son is leasing the mills and a moiety of the lead mines to others. In the seventeenth century, mining was chancy and the part-time work unpopular. The landowners who sold their woods gained in the short term, and the packhorse men, the equivalent of the lorry drivers of the twentieth century, benefited from the transport required. A totally different picture of leadmining developed in the next century.

The High and Low smelt mills at Marrick are still there in the pasture north of Marrick, not as they were in the seventeenth century, for they were rebuilt and used up to the end of mining in the Dales. But perhaps the lower section of the High Mill chimney was that plastered with hair plaster in 1661.

1   Corporation of London Records Office, Guildhall. Survey RCE Sales Contracts, p 315, 1654.

2   Corporation of London Records Office, Guildhall, RCE Committee Minutes, 1632-64, f 185 V; and Royal Contracts M-Y f 117.

3   Based on 'A perfect account from August the first 1657 untill the last of September 1658 both of the leade worke and the other estates of Dr John Bathurst.' MS now lodged at the North Yorkshire County Records Office, Northallerton.

4   PRO E 134 Mich 34 Charles 11 No 25 Yorks. A witness deposes that four bing load and a half of best ore and about five bing load of the worst ore will make a fother of lead and four horse-loads is a bing load of ore. (A bing equals 8 cwt.)

5   PRO E 134 Hilary 25/26 Charles 11 No 20 Yorks. Bathurst v Bathurst; rental for 1658 and also 1675/6, now lodged at the North Yorkshire County Records Office, Northallerton. See also R Fieldhouse and B Jennings, *The History of Richmond and Swaledale* (1978), pp 121, 133-5.

6   L P Wenham, *The History of Richmond School* (1958).

7   Based on 'John Fawcett's Accompt for ye Leade works of Thomas Swinburne at Hurst from November 1660 till ye 24th June 1663'. MS now lodged at the North Yorkshire County Records Office, Northallerton. See also A Raistrick, *The Lead Industries of Wensleydale and Swaledale, Vol II. The Smelting Mills* (1975).

A Seventeenth-Century Leadminer

In the mid-seventeenth century, Thomas Coates, a leadminer, lived at Booze in Arkengarthdale . He was a member of a large family, almost a clan, which more than any other at the time dominated the dale. Coateses lived at the outlying farms of Punchard, Dalehead and Faggergill, and at Sealhouses, Arkle Town and Langthwaite. Then, there were in fact three Thomas and three James Coates.

Bouzes or Bowehouse, as the name has been variously spelt, meaning the house by the bow or curve, is approached by a steep, tortuous road from Langthwaite by the river. Spread across a windswept hillside at 1,100 feet above sea level, scattered houses end in a group of cottages, a farmhouse and many ruins. All around are

The scattered house of Booze, with Slei Gill, scarred by mining, on the right.

Houses at the east of Booze, with Thomas Coate's garth and the ruins of a house behind the farmhouse on the right.

signs of leadmining, bared hillsides, and mining debris in Slei Gill which bounds the place on the west and up to Fell End. Owing to the proximity of the mines, it had forty-one houses in 1851 (and oral tradition relates three inns or beer houses, one with a cockpit). Now there are three occupied farmhouses and seven country cottages. Even in 1676, eleven tenants paid rent for tenements or land at Booze, compared with Langthwaite and Arkle Town down in the valley bottom which had respectively only two and three tenants.[1]

Thomas enjoyed modest means, probably as a younger son taking up mining as an employment. Although described as a miner he was, as was customary, also a farmer, possessing both mining tools and husbandry 'instruments'. Behind Town Farm at the east end of Booze is Thomas Coates's garth, with a ruinous house on the top side and a small garden with straggling gooseberry bushes. But many Coateses lived on after our Thomas's day, and we can only wonder whether this was the site of his house. At any rate we know that he lived on a farm paying a rent of 8s a year. When Dr John Bathurst bought the manor, as we have seen, he immediately raised the rents, and Thomas had his raised to £3 2s a year.[2] But he does not appear to have incurred changes or have been involved in the trials that followed as tenants resisted the changes. That was the fate of some of the better-off such as James Coates of Booze, whose rent was raised from £2 2s 10d to £16 14s 10d.

In a house with three rooms and a lofthouse, Thomas and his wife, Jane, brought up eight children, five boys and three girls: Thomas, Elizabeth, Vincent, John, James, Mary, Margaret, George, This was an example of the large families of those days, usually with many sons. 'Before' the house was a stable and nearby the Oxhouse garths — a rare reference to the former use of oxen in the dales. He had two closes called the Calfehall and the High Close (each with a cowhouse at the head), rights on the common pasture and an intake called Rampshaw. (The latter is about a mile from Booze on the open moor. The name Oxhouse garths is forgotten.)

In 1657, Thomas was working in partnership with three other miners, or 'grouvars' as they were called, in the Lowfield and Eastfield Groves of the then small-scale Bathurst mines, usually avoiding the winter months. From October 1657 to October 1658 he earned £35 8s, his share of ore got in the 'Eastmist shaft', 'a very rich worke ... troubled much with water'. Even so he was in debt to the doctor, as we have seen a common practice. In 1666 he was working in a partnership of two with his eldest son, another Thomas, in a new shaft called Hard Shaft, and that year between them they earned £80 for eighty bing-loads of ore and were out of debt.[3]

Life at Booze must have been harsh in winter but pleasant enough in the long summer days. With the forehouse door open, the family could look south and command a view of the dale, flanked on one side by Fremington Edge and on the other by the long slope of moorland rising up to Calver Hill. Then, Thomas's wet grove clothes could be dried in the sun. Broths and salt meat were boiled in cauldrons hung over an open fire, and furnishings included a great cupboard, perhaps what we now call a court cupboard, and, except for Thomas's, beds were roughly made with most likely a cupboard bed in one of the rooms.

Like most of his contemporaries Thomas was illiterate. But when the time came when he was 'infirm and weake in body', that did not deter him from drafting, on the 27th January 1670, a fair and comprehensive will, remarkable in the circumstances. The will was granted probate in the manor court and was witnessed by William Peacock who made his mark and George Peacock who signed his name with a flourish. Most probably it was George, clerk of the court, who wrote out the will in a beautiful stylish hand.[4]

The eldest son, Thomas, was made executor, and was bequeathed the farm and the husbandry and mining gear. Jane is provided for by leaving her the forehouse and lofthouse for life, after which they revert to Thomas who is left the other two rooms. He has to keep a cow for his mother in winter time and provide pasturage for it 'if she keep a cow'. Jane is left the Oxhouse garths for life, after which they are to be divided equally between the younger sons, Vincent and George. Elizabeth, the eldest daughter, is left £3, a cauldron, a great cupboard, one 'renewed' *why* (heifer),

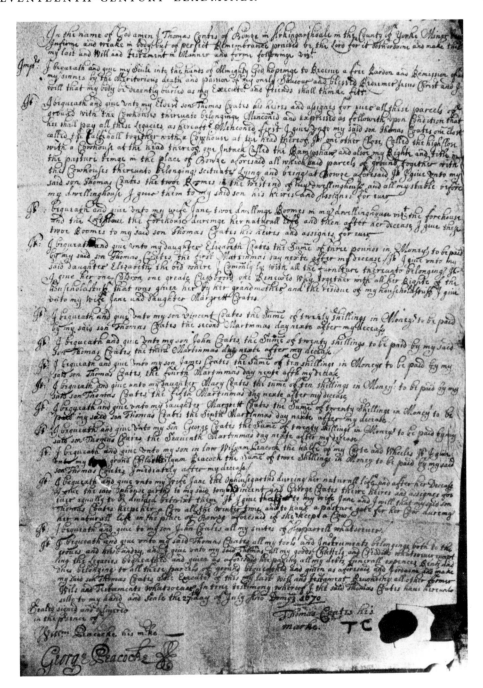

The will of Thomas Coates, leadminer of Booze, Arkengarthdale, 1670.

'the bed where I commonly lie with all the furniture thereunto belonginge', and all the household stuff given her by her grandmother. Jane and another daughter are to share the rest of the household stuff.

Then Thomas followed a form found in a few other wills of the period, which laid the burden of payment on the executor, in this case spread over seven years. Here the legacies were very small. After his death, four of his sons and two daughters are each to be paid by his son, as executor, sums of money in successive years at Martinmas, four of them 20s and two of them 10s. Beginning with Elizabeth, who is to be given her legacy of £3 'the first Martinmas day next after my decease', each year the others follow on in age order until George, the youngest, is paid his legacy of 20s on the 'Seaventh Martinmas day nexte after my decease'. Another son, John, is singled out to have 'all my suites of Apparell'. His son-in-law, William Peacock, has to have 'halfe of my Carte and Wheels' and his grandchild, little William, 2s.

Finally, having apportioned his estate amongst his family as fairly as possible, taking care of his wife but leaving Thomas, his eldest son, a viable inheritance, he signed his will with his mark. Thomas's pious preliminary to his will bequeathes his soul to Almighty God and wills that his body 'be decently buried as his Executor and friends shall think fitt'. When the time came, he would be buried in the churchyard at Arkle Town down by the river where the church formerly stood, and his family and the many Coateses living in the dale would follow him to his grave.

1   Rental, Arkengarthdale, 1675/76. MS now lodged at the North Yorkshire County Records
       Office, Northallerton.
2   Rental, Arkengarthdale, 1658, old and new rents. MS now lodged at the North Yorkshire
       County Records Office, Northallerton.
3   Leadmine accounts, 1657/8 and 1666. MSS now lodged at the North Yorkshire County
       Records Office, Northallerton.
4   Will of Thomas Peacock, 1670. MS now lodged at the North Yorkshire County Records
       Office, Northallerton .

An Eighteenth-Century Parson

The Rev John Dupont was vicar of Aysgarth in Wensleydale for thirty-five stormy years from the 29th October 1733 until he died aged sixty-three on the 22nd December 1768. He stands out above the mediocrity and obscurity of the general run of vicars in remote parishes in those days because in the first place his ancestry, that of victimised Huguenots, and secondly the 1745 Rebellion happening in the midst of his life, acted as a catalyst, galvanising him into writing and publishing.[1] He also lived at a time of change when small churches and parishes in upper Wensleydale were throwing off the yoke of Aysgarth, the mother church, and challenging the vicar's right to the dues and privileges that his forerunners had enjoyed. Disputes were his lot. He was well-educated, vigorous in parochial duties, snobbish, generous, and apparently well-off in later life.

John Dupont came of a family who fled persecution following the repeal of the Edict of Nantes. His grandfather lived at Die, south of Grenoble, and was 'a Person of one of the learned professions', who had officers, their servants and horses quartered on him for a pittance of 5s a day. His household goods were seized and sold, and his wife and his children dispersed for safety until opportunity for flight and voluntary exile presented themselves.

César and Susannah Dupont, John's parents, came to live at Middleham in lower Wensleydale, possibly joining a group of fellow *emigrés*. Their son was sent to the grammar school at Kirkleatham, near Redcar, recently founded by Sir William Turner. Thence at the age of twenty he was admitted pensioner to Trinity College, Cambridge, where he matriculated, became a scholar and took his BA in 1728-29. He was ordained deacon, then priest, and was appointed to the curacy of Gildern Morden, Cambridgeshire. He married Frances Jeffreys, daughter of the rector of Wimpole in the same county, and shortly became his father-in-law's curate there. At Wimpole three of his children were baptized, one of them after the move to Aysgarth.[2]

Meanwhile his father had bought Temple Dowskar, a large, rambling old house so called after its links with the Knights Templars, near Swinithwaite between Aysgarth and West Witton. César transferred the property to his son, probably on his marriage. So, when John Dupont was offered the vicarage of Aysgarth by the Master and Fellows of his old college, Trinity, who had the gift of the living and were the impropriators of the tithes, he came to live at Temple and was inducted at Aysgarth on the 29th October 1733.

Here he lived at any rate, as time went on, in some style, bringing up three sons and three daughters. His mind he tells us was 'most intimately engaged and taken up with the anxious Cares and Inspection of a numerous and growing Family'. His sons, Francis, John and Joseph, chose careers in the army. (Three of his nearest relations, he also tells us, bore arms under William III in his foreign wars and at the Battle of the Boyne, where a contingent of Huguenots fought on the king's side.) His stipend as vicar was £39 a year, plus some dues and the farm of Aysgarth's huge churchyard. His father gave him a pension of £200 a year, and later John Dupont paid the same sum for land at West Witton to add to the glebe. Besides these the stipend was augmented by Queen Anne's Bounty, and as was usual amongst the enterprising in those days, he joined with two partners in a profitable leadmining venture at Woodhall, near Askrigg.

The old house at Temple Dowskar had a new front added in the Georgian period, but whether before or after John Dupont's sojourn is not clear. A barn close to, originally a two-storied coach house, was evidently built by him, having the initials and date JDF 1761 on a keystone of an arch. The rooms were well furnished — one had a repeating clock and a large looking glass, and his study contained a 'library of books'. Silver spoons, salvers and pint mugs graced his table, and there was a brewhouse, and a large wine cellar with an arched roof, still there. The garden, too, still has a ha-ha, a walled kitchen garden and an orchard.

John Dupont was more English than the English, fulsomely praising in his writings his adopted country and the Hanoverians, including the Duke of Cumberland. One of his first moves as vicar was to have the king's arms painted, framed and hung up in the church, an undertaking costing £24 10s 8d. Later, when he proposed that the bells be rung annually to celebrate the king's birthday, for which the ringers were to be paid 5s, he had one of his brushes with a group of parishioners who disapproved of a 'Novel Expense' which they 'had been unwarily drawn into by ye Vicar's Loyal Proposal'.[3] No doubt his parishioners soon came to know their vicar's phobias.

Only four years after his induction, there arose a dispute about the re-pewing of Aysgarth church following the building of a vestry by an unpopular lord of the manor. The third verse of one of John Dupont's poems *The Cabal* reads:

> *A Vestry he's made, and his ambitious views*
> *Will need metamorphose our good Stalls into Pews;*
> *And in Truth should his Credit increase with the People,*
> *Next year he'd persuade them to alter the Steeple.*
> > *Derry down, down …*

Nonetheless, in 1741—43 the church was re-pewed, including removing and altering the pulpit.

Temple, the home of the Rev John Dupont, showing the eighteenth-century front and the ha-ha in the foreground.

His was without doubt a contentious nature, although in mitigation it must be said that independence was in the air, in particular at Hawes and Stalling Busk, chapelries carved out of the original parish of Aysgarth. In both these, Dupont became involved in disputes over the right of the nomination of incumbents. At Hawes the matter was resolved by the arbitration of the Bishop of Chester, in whose diocese were then both chapelries, who decided in favour of the inhabitants. At Stalling Busk a long drawn-out quarrel ensued, complicated by Dupont's claim to retain the licence to perform burials and marriages at Busk. Again in the end, after letters had shuttled to and fro from both sides to the bishop, he finally came down on the side of the inhabitants.

A few years later in the 1750s, as a trustee of Yorebridge Grammar School founded in 1601 at Askrigg, Dupont was once more involved, this time in a more serious dispute when the trustees (led by Thomas Metcalfe of Nappa Hall, whose side he was on) clashed with the heirs-at-law of the founder over the appointment of a master. The case, taken before the court of Chancery in 1754—58, resulted in victory for the trustees but also in severe monetary loss.

Aysgarth Church as it was in the Rev John Dupont's day before the nineteenth-century restoration. Note the huge churchyard.

But twelve years after he came to Aysgarth, the 1745 Rebellion shattered the peace of his retreat, especially when the Young Pretender, marching south, passed within a few miles of his parish. Although he had been writing poems, essays, and making translations since his student days, this event sent him hastening in alarm to pen and paper, for 'everything that was dear and valuable to me as a PROTESTANT SUBJECT was at stake'.

Part of his vehemence arose from an accident, for when sounds of gunshot were heard at Hawes, ten miles away, in one of the slight skirmishes as the Scottish army passed, the vicar was laid up with a broken leg 'which', he wrote, 'prevented me from exerting myself in my Parish and Neighbourhood with that becoming Zeal and Activity, which in that time of common danger every true PROTESTANT was obliged to express. Stung to the soul with the affected supineness of some, and the real Indolence and Stupidity of others, I undertook to expose the traiterous Knavery and Wickedness of these ... more especially after the unfortunate Affair of Preston Pans ... Twas at that Crisis I commenc'd Author in the Cause of Religion my

King and Country, and printed off and dispersed as Essay called *An Address to all True Englishmen*.' This was printed at York for John Hildyard, Bookseller, Stonegate, in 1745.

On Sunday the 10th November 1745 he fulminated in a sermon preached at Aysgarth 'How little are [Protestants] acquainted with the barbarous and bloody Spirit and Principles of the Church of Rome', and he pronounced 'The French, the Antient and most inveterate enemies of this Nation.'

Although there was only one true Popish family in his parish and another 'of very small consideration', it was no wonder that he provoked trouble and that 'a sturdy Fellow was sent soon after to my House, who threatened me with having my throat cut, and being afterwards hung up at my Door'.

In its catalogue the British Library lists six items under Dupont's name, but some are single sermons, all of which are contained in his two books *The Loyal Miscellany, Consisting of Several Sermons and other Tracts and Essays in Prose and Verse published in separate Pieces from the Beginning of the late Unnatural Rebellion, to the Conclusion of the present Peace*, published for the author by T Read in Dogwell Court, White Frier, in 1751. A *Second Volume of Miscellanies consisting of Sermons and other Essays* was printed at York by N Nickson in Feasegate in 1767.

The first volume written in the heat of the moment is the most interesting. He dedicates it to his Royal Highness William, Duke of Cumberland, without reservations his hero for the suppression of the rebellion at Culloden. The second is dedicated to the Right Honourable Thomas, Earl of Kinnoul, whose chaplain he became.

He takes advantage of prefaces to pursue his favourite themes, and he published sermons given at Aysgarth on days set apart for public thanksgivings or general fasts. Only one, given on a Good Friday, is purely religious. In May 1746, after the victory at Culloden, he preached on 'Rebellion and Treachery defeated by Bravery and Conduct'. 'To be influenc'd and inflam'd with a true love of our Country,' he proclaimed, 'is a great and noble Passion.' The Aysgarth church bells were rung both in 1745 and after Culloden. On the 9th October 1746 his sermon enlarged on 'the Peculiar Happiness and Excellency of the British Nation consider'd and explain'd', in which quoting the constitution, wise laws, the church, 'the Glory of the Christian World', he says 'we are [in many instances] preferable and superior to every other People'.

In spite of his verbosity and immodesty, a fair knowledge of ancient and modern history is apparent. On Friday the 11th February 1757 he preached a sermon in a different vein on 'National Corruption and Depravity the principal Cause of National Disappointments', in which he attacked atheism, those who have made a schism in the church (Wesleyans), sabbath breakers, gin drinking, and the fashions and fopperies of the French.

He even takes it upon himself to write 'The Country Clergyman's Advice to the People of Great Britain in General. But more especially to the opulent and flourishing

Inhabitants of the Cities of London and Westminster.' One complaint is that goods and merchandise are being manufactured 'in a certain variegated Figure and Form [presumably tartan] as cannot but be disagreeable to those you ought to honour and reverence'. He also suggests that they 'ferrit out those incendiary Locusts of the Church of Rome'.

Signing himself 'The son of a French Protestant', he wrote letters and sent poems to the *Newcastle Journal,* a paper then taken locally, and the *General Evening Post* and St *James's Chronicle.* In one letter he put forward the suggestion that anyone showing bravery in battle should be allowed to wear a shoulder knot or an imitation of a sprig of laurel on public occasions. In another he praises 'a genuine Liberty which issues from God' and not 'unbounded Licentiousness'. He adds 'The Subject I have pitch'd upon is so very copious and fruitful that I cannot without trespassing too much on your Indulgence, and the Reader's Patience, crowd all my Thoughts upon it in one, and shall therefore trouble you with the Sequel in another Letter'.

His poetry had best be passed over quickly. In the second volume he included early work and apologised for the 'gayer cast' of some of the poems, pleading that 'they were wrote when I was young and full of spirits'. His subjects are 'Night', a few on the charms of women, the shade of Alexander Pope, an execrable epigram on Laurence Sterne, the Duke of Cumberland's birthday, one in Latin on the death of George II, 'A eulogium of the Pipe from the French', and one which deplores the destruction of the deer in a certain park. Names are omitted and innuendo rather than plain fact distinguish his writings, so that little is to be learnt from them of local interest. The poem on the deer gives the briefest glimpse of life at Temple on the occasion of the annual celebration of West Witton Feast, called after the patron saint of the church there, St Bartholomew, shortened to Bartle:

> *Besides (the Shoe here pinches sore)*
> *We ne'er shall taste of Ven'son more,*
> *When Guests are seated at our Table,*
> *At Bartle's Feast we shan't be able*
> *To say, this Shoulder's fine and fat,*
> *Oh Sir! oh Madam! pray taste of that;*

In the second volume he touches on a variety of subjects, piqued that it had been assumed that his interests were limited. He is certainly aggrieved, writing that 'Upon the Whole then, the Author has suffered too much in his Character — by injurious and false Reports, to pass them over altogether unnoticed', and he all too humanly remarks: 'As every Man who produces himself to the world as an Author, cannot but entertain some favourable Prejudices of his Performance.' 372 people subscribed to the second volume, including the Master of the Rolls, the Speaker of the House of Commons, the Hon Edward Montague of Berkeley Square, many dignitaries from Edinburgh and Grantham, and all the parsons and everyone of note in the immediate and more distant neighbourhoods.

As an author, John Dupont also excuses his shortcomings by pleading that he 'was frequently employ'd in the necessary Duties and Avocations of a very extensive Parish (which 'tis humbly presum'd, have been faithfully discharged)'. Once he writes of being in London on matters of concern to his family. But what the connection with Edinburgh was is not explained. At the time of his father's death, Joseph was serving an apprenticeship, probably in the army. Francis, the eldest son and the executor of his will, fought from 1757 to 1765 in the East Indies in a series of sieges and battles, including the capture of Manila from the Spaniards.[4]

When John Dupont died, he left his wife, Frances, the little parlour with a chamber and garret over, the red room, the shaving room, a little cellar, furniture and utensils, the use of the kitchen, cellar and brewhouse, as well as a share of the garden and its fruit 'so long as she continues my widow'. Frances had her own gold watch and a pearl necklace.[5] He left £50 and 5 guineas apiece to his daughter, Elizabeth, and her husband, John Forster, to buy mourning. His second daughter, Susannah, had £100 in addition to another £100 given to her by her godfather, the Hon Rev John Wandesford, also silver, furniture, and 'my own gold watch'. His younger children, John, Frances and Joseph each received £100, and a small sum was left to the poor of the parish.

John Dupont rounded off his wishes by ordering his son, Francis, to sell his library of books and to share the proceeds amongst his six children, and 'to burn all the loose papers which he shall find in my study or elsewhere in my said dwelling house'. He was buried in the church, but after the restoration of the last century, the gravestone was placed outside near the south wall of the chancel next to his mother's. It bears the inscription that 'he was an unknown loss to his friends and a great benefactor to the poor'.

Dupont was no literary figure to compare with his fellow Yorkshire clergymen, Laurence Sterne and Sydney Smith, but he surely deserves a niche in the annals of his adopted country.

1   Based on John Dupont's *The Loyal Miscellany* (1751) and *A Second Volume of Miscellanies consisting of Sermons and other Essays* (1767), loaned to us from Wensleydale School.
2   Cambridge CRO G/1/11 and A1518 and University Archives, University Library, Cambridge EDR G1/11, ff 286, 297, 312.
3   NYCRO PR/AYS/3/1, Aysgarth Churchwardens Accounts .
4   Information kindly given by Mr C T Dupont of Montreal.
5   Will of John Dupont, 1768. York Minster Library.

Base Metal

That greed and envy were motivating factors in leadmining in the Dales is without doubt, and the disputes leading to court cases concerning the mines, especially those in the eighteenth century as mining expanded and before boundaries had been clarified, were both numerous and lengthy. By now leadmining held out great promise of reward and for the miners themselves, paid wages of a shilling a shift or taking bargains to search independently for lead, it had become a full-time job. In Swaledale in particular, men were prone to litigation. A major dispute in the late eighteenth century illustrates how far these quarrels could be carried, and as a side issue reveals much about life and farming in earlier centuries.

A mile from Keld at the head of Swaledale are the ruins of the farmhouse, Crackpot Hall. West of it rises up the gouged-out hillsides and spoil heaps of the one-time Beldy Hill leadmine on Crackpot Hall out-pasture, and east of it the ravine of Swinnergill, devastated by mining and with the ruins of two smelt mills, one at the mouth of the gill and another higher up near East Grain. This almost totally deserted place was once the scene of furious mining activity and angry exchanges between rival factions. It was reached from the west by a bridge over the Swale and across East Gill from Keld, and from the east by the old road from Gunnerside and Low Row via Calvert Houses on the north side of Swaledale. Along this track, especially before winter, came packhorses on the way to Tan Hill coal pits, and along it too in the eighteenth century came miners, agents, boys and women washers, gangs of packhorses, witnesses in the trials and the curious.[1]

The drama begins in 1738 when that part of the estates of Philip, Duke of Wharton, the manors of Healaugh and Muker, were sold for £10,500 to Thomas Smith of Easby, described at the time of the trials as a lawyer of Gray's Inn and a recluse who seldom left his chambers. The mineral rights on the commons and wastes were excluded from the sale — the crucial clause — but with them went the rights for the whole gamut of mining: the erection of buildings, cottages, mills, forges, engines, the making of watercourses and ways to carry goods, the right to take stones and clods for the repair of buildings, and to carry away peat. This digest of the agreement describes what was to happen at Beldy Hill and in Swinnergill.

At the time of the sale to Thomas Smith the leadmines yielded a considerable

Crackpot Hall in the 1950s, before it had to be abandoned owing to mining subsidence.

revenue, out of which the Duchess of Wharton received an annuity, and the residue went to the sister of the Duke, Lady Jane Coke, who died in 1760. She left her estates to Anna Maria Draycott, whom she had brought up, and who four years later married George, the second Earl of Pomfret, an extravagant and impetuous character. The first earl, his father and his mother had enjoyed an extensive and prolonged Grand Tour, and on succeeding to the title in 1753 he had become heir to many treasures, some of which he sold to pay debts. At the time of the marriage the profits of the mines had diminished.

In the 1740s a partnership of local men — Leonard Hartley of Middleton Tyas near Richmond, and two brothers, John and Thomas Parke of Low Row, Swaledale (John was a miner and Thomas a hosier, that is a middle man in the knitting industry) — had taken leases of ground for mining at various places in the upper dale from Smith's agent. There were two leases for twenty-one years, dated 1742 and 1743, covering ground from West Stonesdale to Swinnergill including Crackpot Hall.[2]

The site of Lord Pomfret's smelt mill in East Grain, Swinnergill.

It was in the second lease that Crackpot Hall out-pasture (which included Beldy Hill) was specifically mentioned. Eventually the dire quarrel was to turn on whether Crackpot Hall out-pasture belonged to the farm and thus to Mr Smith, or was on the commons where the mineral rights belonged to Lord Pomfret. His lordship's faction never in fact called it the out-moor, but Hall Edge or Hall Moor.

The Hartley/Parke partnership began mining at once, but failing at Beldy Hill they moved to that side of the ground near to Swinnergill. Here in time up to forty men were employed in sinking shafts, often working on Sundays, and three sets of pumps were manned night and day. They were so troubled by water that in 1749 they drove a low drainage level, to be known as Parke's level, at a cost of £300. On the opposite side of Swinnergill, distant from each other by only 150 or 200 yards, another group of miners were at work for the Wharton trustees. Strict demarcation by dialling had to be marked out. It became apparent that the new level would also drain the mines of the rivals across the gill. However, when the Parkes' mine became unproductive they asked the Wharton's agent, James Close, for a consideration to keep the drainage level open. This was refused, with the result that they stopped up the level and drowned out their rivals. Naturally, bad feeling resulted.

Meanwhile, by 1767 John and Thomas Parke had died, and the sons of Thomas, John and Ralph (both bachelors), joined with Leonard Hartley in a new lease and continued successful mining. They had already sublet ten meers (thirty-two yards of ground on the vein of lead) in 1765 to Richard Metcalfe of Calvert Houses, John Scott, a shopkeeper of Reeth, and their partners, and shortly afterwards this group struck a very promising vein at Beldy Hill. In eighteen months they had raised 1,300 bing of ore. (A bing was eight hundredweight of dressed ore) . The news flashed round the dale in no time.

The rivals on the other side of Swinnergill were not doing well. Lord Pomfret, recently married to the owner of the royalties, now enters the scene. He was in debt. New agents were appointed and the stage was set for a major clash. Egged on by William I'Anson of Leyburn, agent and attorney, and John Metcalfe of Dykeheads near Gunnerside, Lord Pomfret filed a bill in Chancery in 1768 claiming that the Beldy Hill mine was on part of the commons that is on his property and not part of Crackpot Hall farm owned by Thomas Smith. He failed to obtain an injunction to restrain his opponents from working there, but that was only the beginning.

Inevitably the farm, its tenants, and especially the extent and boundaries of the out-pasture figured prominently in the trials that followed. Today, anyone who knew the hall before it fell into ruin thinks of its grand position high above the Swale, a fitting scenario for the drama enacted there and the characters who once lived at it. From the memorandum books or diaries kept by John Parke, depositions of witnesses and documents relating to the trials that followed, a picture may be built up of farming and life in Swaledale at the time.

From about the mid-seventeenth century, Crackpot Hall was occupied by

The ruins of Beldy Hill smelt mill, at the mouth of Swinnergill.

members of the Harker family, of whom Edmond Harker, who died aged seventy-two in 1709, had been employed by the old Lord Wharton as keeper of the red deer, and from time to time he had killed one for his lordship's use. In that part of Hall out-pasture near to East Gill there was once two closes, High Gill Close and Low Gill Close; and in the latter stood the ruins of Gill House, containing a forehouse and parlour, and with the remains of outbuildings and small enclosures, reputed to have once been occupied by the keeper of the red deer. Deer were only just fading in memory as part of the scene.

What remained of woodland round Crackpot Hall is hard to determine. To this day the birch, ash and thorn of ancient forest clothe both sides of the Swale gorge, but everywhere else is bare. There was a wood at West Stonesdale, and no doubt many more trees and scrub dotted the fells, with yews in the gills and thorns widespread. A Giles Metcalfe who chopped wood for the smelt mills is described as a woodcutter for Lord Wharton. But in the 1760s, mine timber and buddle boards were often brought from Westmorland, and in 1758 a massive piece of oak, presumably for an axle-tree for a waterwheel, was carried at great expense from Wetherby Grange, some seventy miles away, to upper Swaledale.

In 1690 Edmond's son, Simon Harker, or Guy Simon as he was called, followed his father as tenant of Crackpot Hall and remained there for fifty years. He occupied an older house than the present ruin, with another dwelling adjoining it. On the 27th April 1704, he married Jane Metcalfe of Sedbusk in Wensleydale at Askrigg Church. During their married life they usually employed a maid servant and a man servant who were often relatives, and sometimes took in a boarder. Simon paid £20 a year rent for the farm of 150 acres plus the 240 acres of the out-pasture which had been enclosed in 1635. In time his son, another Edmond, and his wife lived with them, but Edmond died in 1731. Nine years later, Simon moved to Calvert Houses, dying there in 1750 long before the time of the trials. But his reputation lived after him.

When he followed his father at Crackpot Hall, the boundary fence of the out-pasture was in poor shape, and he asked the duke's agent to have it put up. But instead it was suggested that he repair it himself, a proposition to which he agreed if allowed a year's rent. But this was refused. However, for his own sake to save himself hounding his sheep, he patched it up, cobbling up the walls and 'bearding' them, that is putting thorns on top, then a common practice. He also bearded with thorns and other wood the clefts between the rocks on the Swinnergill side.

On the out-pasture, Simon kept sheep and cattle. At one time a Thomas Johnson boarded with him. Johnson used to buy wether hoggs (male lambs) at Whitsuntide at Brough Fair, pay Simon for pasturage, and sell them in November at Middleham Moor Fair. Noting that this paid off, Simon went into partnership with Johnson, but they fell out over the expense of driving them to market. Occasionally, to stock the pasture Simon bought 'a great number of calves' at either Stokesley or Guisborough fairs.

In summer time the pasture was herded and hounded with diligence, but it was not worthwhile doing so in winter. It was only valued at nine pence an acre and was described as 'the most barren spot in the Kingdom'. One of the boundary marks, Raven's or Buzzard's Nest, indicates its extent and wildness. In early summer Simon dug a supply of peats at his peat pot there, and once when burning ling prior to cutting he nearly set the commons on fire. Here, too, he agisted other people's stock, often horses for which men took a summergate at sixpence a week. One man who went to fetch his horse failed to find it at once, as the animal had strayed across six or more miles of moorland to Spittle Houses on Stainmore.

Around Crackpot other tenants, men from East and West Stonesdale, Calvert Houses, Ivelet and Winterings (above Gunnerside), had their sheep heafs or heughs, that is parts of the commons where the lambs had grown up with their mothers and so stayed there. From time to time their sheep strayed on to the in- and out-pastures of Crackpot Hall Farm. Simon either demanded money for the trespass, or frequently set his dogs on them so roughly that they were driven over the scars of Swinnergill and broke their backs. If he was away, he even ordered his maid servant to hound off stray sheep.

On occasions, loud altercations echoed over the hills. Simon and another neighbour were described as 'honest men but very hasty in passion'. Some had problems, for they had bought sheep and lambs (at a shilling and sixpence apiece) from Simon and they instinctively returned to their old pastures. Others came to terms with the trouble by buying Simon a drink, and one, Edward Simpson, gave him a beastgate in Ivelet pasture in return for clemency.

The Metcalfes, living at Craketrees (the farm, Crow Trees, at the foot of the Oxnop Pass into Swaledale), entered into an agreement with him, paying Simon two shillings and sixpence a year so as not to have their sheep dogged, and in addition they invited him and his wife to their feasts in order 'to keep kind with him'.

Driven to desperation, the tenants met together in a great assembly to consider bringing an action against Simon. It did not materialise, but they 'Begged he would snap only one dog, and drive their sheep more tenderly'. This 'extremely cross and sturdy' defence of his territory naturally featured as important testimony to prove that Hall out-pasture belonged to the farm. Not surprisingly, several members of the Harker clan appeared as witnesses.

In 1740 when a new tenant, George Metcalfe, took over, it was under the new landlord, Thomas Smith, who had employed an improving agent. The rent was raised to £26 a year and the fence of the out-pasture repaired. Two men were employed to erect drystone walls at a shilling a rood, and two more to build earth and sod fences with gutters on either side at nearly sixpence a rood. To follow the original line of the sod fence they took old Simon Harker with them. In all, 184 roods of wall were built at a cost of £9 14s and 172 roods of sod fence at £4 2s 11d. George Metcalfe had the misfortune to have the out-pasture stocked with cattle at the time of the murrain raging over the country from 1747 to 1753, and he lost many beasts.

This was the background to the dispute. In his diaries John Parke sticks closely to the day-to-day moves. He hardly mentions a third brother, Thomas, who then lived in Wensleydale, and he never describes his home life beyond referring to the numerous people who called with news at his house, Gorton Lodge, in Low Row. Very many local names appear in the diaries: Alderson, Broderick, Metcalfe, Raw, Coates, Rutter, Reynoldson, Harker, Kearton. John records the endless journeys to Beldy Hill, the constant enquiries about the boundaries, the rumours that circulated, and the violence that was perpetrated. For four years most people in Swaledale, and some in Wensleydale and Westmorland, became embroiled in the bitter feud either as participants, witnesses or as purveyors of news and gossip.

Swaledale was then a very different place from what it is now. Both Reeth and Muker markets were in full swing. New leadmines were continually being opened, and the knitting industry still flourished. Industrial enterprises enabled fortunes to be made in the dale itself. The Parkes were involved in both the knitting and the leadmining trades, and the Hartleys in lead and coppermining. Leonard Hartley's cousin, George, always referred to as Lawyer Hartley, practised as a barrister in

Reeth in 1978.

Richmond and was continually consulted. Another contemporary, Caleb Readshaw, many times mayor of Richmond, was both a merchant/hosier and a lessee of lead and copper mines, whilst the Robinsons of Stockton were agents who bought and sold lead.

These entrepreneurs of the eighteenth century are recorded dining together at the King's Head in Richmond, spoken of as Mr Forrest's. There were James Stodart, Thomas Smith's agent, Dr Wright and other Richmond worthies, besides Alexander Fothergill, lawyer and turnpike surveyor from Wensleydale who is mentioned in the Parke diary. More than once John records casual meetings and the exchange of news at the cockpit behind the King's Head. The Parkes also bought books and a quire of paper for Thomas Butson, their local agent living at Keld, from Robert Tinkler, bookseller of Pinfold Green, Richmond, and no doubt the memorandum books, stitched down the middle and backed with rough brown paper, came from the same source.[3] Robert was the husband of Tibby (Isabella) Tinkler, whose portrait was engraved by George Cuitt, artist of Richmond. She died aged ninety-two in 1794.

Up and down the dale, horse traffic seldom ceased, from single riders to gangs (or sets) of packhorses carrying wood to the mines, lead ore to the smelt mills or

Isabella ('Tibby') Tinkler, bookseller of Richmond, a portrait by George Cuitt.

pigs of lead to Hartforth on their way to Stockton. Some of the Scotch Galloways used were bred in the dale at Low Row, and others at Hope, over the moors north of Arkengarthdale. Packhorses here are always called Galloways, from their origin in lowland Scotland where they were once a distinct breed and related to the Fell and Dales ponies. They were about fourteen hands, often brown with black legs, and noted for their stamina. On one journey, each horse is recorded carrying 22 st 5 lb of lead ore in pokes (as we have seen in bags made of harden) supported on pack saddles. Two pigs of lead made a pony-load. Bad harvests and poor corn affected the horses adversely, slowing down their rate of travel.

The jaggers who owned and drove them — James Galloway, James Cherry, Robert White, Chris Naylor and others — usually had about nine horses, sometimes more, and the forehorse wore a special collar marked with the owner's initials. (Bells are not actually mentioned, although in his *Romantic Richmondshire* of 1897, Speight says: 'When the packhorse traffic ceased, hundreds of these sonorous packhorse bells were sold for old metal, and the brokers' shops for a time were full of them.'[4]) A few years previously in 1762, James Galloway had witnessed a tragic accident when going with lead to Hartforth with another jagger. This man, riding aside and falling asleep on his horse on the return journey, fell off backwards and subsequently died.

The first entry in John Parke's memoranda records one of the early moves in the dispute, a move which followed directly from the failure of the bill in Chancery to restrain the Metcalfe partnership from working. On Monday the 5th June 1769, Lord Pomfret's men, led by his agent I'Anson and others, took the law into their own hands and 'Begun to work at Beldy Hill near to the Hush, that when they broke ground they drank a Bottle of Brandy and began Huzzaing'. The next day the Parkes went there with 'a number of Whitaside Miners' to view the situation. They found the invaders sinking shafts and discharged them from working there to no avail. A week later they started to sink a new shaft themselves, organised by Thomas Butson, and they plied their thirty-six workers with ale at sixpence a head.

So the entries continue, revealing the inflammable situation of them all sinking shafts close to each other. Smith, Hartley and Parkes filed a cross bill to restrain the invaders from working there. In October, Lord Pomfret applied to the court at York asking for an injunction to stop Metcalfe and partners working. He obtained a decree pending trial at York of the case allowing the parties to work the mine, but all monies accruing to be placed in the bank at three per cent. His party had successfully continued mining for four months.

On the 23rd July 1769, John Parke wrote: 'Isaac Alderson told me that when John Metcalfe enter'd upon Spout Gill Mill [where most of the lead from Beldy Hill was smelted] it was computed there was then in and about the said Mill 500 Bings of Ore & Slaggs both to the value of about 2000 Pounds.'

On Wednesday the 27th September of the same year, Lord Pomfret journeyed north by post chaise and accompanied by Justice Chaytor and his agent I'Anson arrived at Beldy Hill. John Parke entered in his diary: 'Lord P—t came there & Stood on the hill Top for some Time near to some Ore rais'd by Scott and partn^s & then he and the rest of the Compan^y, along with him went to view the Fences belonging to the pasture ... he then return'd ... and called on me and gave me a Discharge by word of Mouth from working there ...' The Rev Mr Emerson, Thomas Smith's brother-in-law, who was also there, in turn discharged his lordship. It was a stormy day and a lively scene. Lord Pomfret had had brought in many packhorses to carry away the ore he had won (eventually valued at £1,334 15s) so that miners, washers and jaggers were at work amidst the crowd.

Another typical entry reports the beginnings of local troubles:

> 'Oct 9 1769, about 3 oclock in the morning Jas Close's Son came to my house & inform'd Bro Ralph that Ld P—t's Men had turned the Water into the Shafts, Bro Ralph went the same day to B^y Hill & was inform'd by David Brunskill that when he attempted to turn of the said Water Thos Waller threw him ... into the Hush Gutter ... This Day Joseph Close of Crackpot Hall inform'd me that John Metcalfe of Dikeheads had rec^d a Letter from L^d P—t since his L^{d}ship went away — that they were to do all the Mischief they cou'd & I think he likewise said his L^{d}ship wou'd protect them.'

As the months passed, Lord Pomfret's men attacked Thomas Smith's property in earnest. The weir and water race of the newly-built Raygill Mill, eight miles from Beldy Hill on Old Gang Beck, were damaged, repaired and damaged again and again. The bellows were burnt until at length they were brought to safety each night to save watching over them. Smith's Spout Gill Mill in the Oxnop valley off Swaledale changed hands by force and by stratagem. Men of the opposing factions fought underground and, because of water turned into the shafts to drown out their rivals, the Parkes fitted trap doors with locks and bolts to four of them. Others overthrew stacks and stamps (small stacks) of hay and eased themselves on them.

Lord Pomfret's men, often in bands of as many as fourteen, behaved with surprising violence in their employer's interest, sometimes lured on by promised favours, sometimes bearing grudges against the Smith side for supposed ill-treatment, but in general, with ill feeling escalating, plainly spoiling for a fight. They did not escape scot free, but were arrested and brought before Justice Fielding in the dale and William Chaytor at Spennithorne in Wensleydale, a lawyer and a prominent participant on the side of Lord Pomfret in the trial, and in leadmining in general. At one time or another some appeared at Thirsk sessions, some paid small fines, some were sent to the House of Correction in Richmond, one to York Castle. Fourteen stood trial at the assizes at York. Others fled into Westmorland eventually to return 'disenchanted'. After a hearing at York, Thomas Smith was awarded £400 damages.

Other entries describe moving the ore from Beldy Hill to claim it and the surveying of the out-pasture by both parties. Thomas Butson with others measured the fences in February 1770, and a plan of Crackpot Hall Farm showing the

A page from John Parke's diary for the 26th to 28th September 1769. It records the arrival of Lord Pomfret at Beldy Hill.

Old Curly, a Swaledale leadminer. There was a 'Curly Dick' mentioned in the Parke diary. He was John Metcalfe, a smelter at Spout Gill smelt mill.

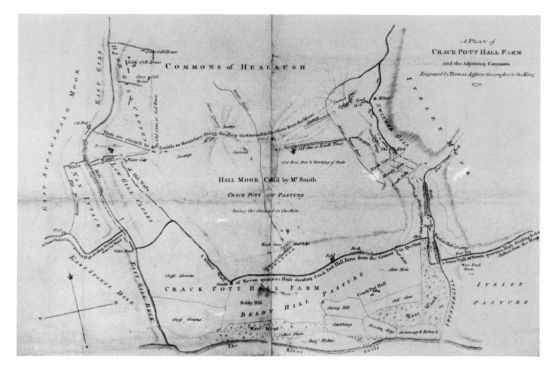

A plan of Crackpot Hall Farm engraved by Thomas Jefferys in 1772, probably commissioned by Lord Pomfret. It shows the boundaries of Hall out-pasture with the 'Mines in Question' above Beldy Hill; also Low Gill Closes, within the pasture next to East Gill Beck with 'Ruins of House', presumably Gill House mentioned in the trials; and north of this, on the commons, High Gill Closes with Great Gill House, Eddy Gill House and Sievy Gill House in it. The road to the Tan Hill pits runs close to the River Swale.

out-pasture was engraved by Thomas Jefferys, the cartographer, in 1772.[5] It was noted that Adam Alderson, schoolmaster of Angram, had been to view the pasture. Women washers were given a shilling for drink, as were the jaggers, and one man who asked to go down one of the Parke's shafts was lent a candle and 'a Sute of Grove clothes'.

The then tenant of Crackpot Hall, Joseph Close, who had followed Metcalfe and a Ralph Scott, was paid ten shillings and sixpence for damage done to his farm by mining, and his wife earned five shillings for 2,000 stop-rods (wood for wattling the shaft of a mine) and took in lodgers. Joseph, too, hounded his neighbours' sheep too roughly. Even sheep marks are recorded in the diary: A Sword on the Far Side, a Pop on the near Hook bone, a Crow's Foot on the Buttock, a Door Stapple, and mention is made of 'Mr Smith's clippings' as if these were great gatherings at specific folds.

Meanwhile Richard Metcalfe, John Scott and partners withheld the payment of forty shillings a fother due to Hartley and Parkes for the lead they had got, and later argued as to whether their bargain included mill and millage, that is the use of the smelt mill. They perfidiously entered into an agreement with Lord Pomfret so that if he won they would be on the right side. At one point, when John Scott persistently eluded the Parkes, they knocked at his door in Reeth in the early hours of the morning to demand either the money due or an account of it, but Scott let his maid servant ward them off. It was assessed in 1768 that Metcalfe and Scott owed Hartley and Parkes between £1,700 and £1,800. Nonetheless, in 1770-71 the Parkes built a smelt mill at the foot of Swinnergill and a cart road costing £50 leading to it from Beldy Hill.

Whilst these sordid local quarrels continued, the main trials took place. In May 1768, Lord Pomfret had exhibited his bill in Chancery, and in October 1769 he applied to the court at York for an injunction to stop Metcalfe and his partners working the mine. The trial came on at York at the summer assizes in 1770 before a special jury, when the verdict was found for Thomas Smith. In 1771, for a second hearing in Chancery, a commission took depositions of witnesses at Kirkby Stephen, Richmond and Barnard Castle. Next year a third hearing in Chancery in June was followed by the great trial at the court of the King's Bench in London.

John Parke has very little to say about these, and a day that one of the hearings in Chancery came on, the 16th November 1771, he wrote 'The Greatest Flood that ever was known in the Memory of Man' had befallen Swaledale. But people were constantly setting forward to York or London. (Ralph Parke's expenses to and from London in 1769 were £27 2s 3d), and, for Thomas Smith, lawyers' fees and the transport of witnesses proved very costly. The jurors were members of the northern gentry and some had to view the ground in dispute. It is recorded that the trial in London on a Saturday, the 7th November 1772, continued all day for fourteen hours for the examination of Lord Pomfret's witnesses, and that it was with difficulty that Lord Mansfield, the judge, was persuaded to postpone it until the Monday, although many of Thomas Smith's witnesses were very old and tired and had had nothing to eat.

In the end the verdict was found for Thomas Smith. The argument in his favour by Alexander Wedderburn, the Solicitor General, was masterly. On the 25th November 1773, only three years later and at the age of eighty, Thomas Smith died at Grays Inn. Lord Pomfret had been indefatigable. He had forced the trials; he had appealed to the House of Lords three times; and he was at one point in the Tower of London for debt. Much later, when he was old and infirm, he was in trouble with his leadmine agents and had granted an unreasonably wide lease of land on Gunnerside Beck. He died in 1785.

As for the Parkes, the last but one entry in the memoranda reads: 'Saturday, Aug 22 1772 Mr Smith and Lawyer Hartley both thought it proper that we should begin

Afternoon drinkings at Crackpot Hall: Ernest and Margaret Harker, and Alice (1932).

to work the mines at Beldy Hill.' John Parke died in 1796 aged seventy-three, leaving Ralph to carry on. They had already become less active. Perhaps John was failing and Ralph, when his brother died, lacked support; for in February 1802 the new owner of the royalties, another Thomas Smith, wrote: 'It gave me great pleasure to hear the Lessees of Beldy Hill are at length awakening from their nine years profound sleep.'[6] Ralph died in 1811.

The third brother, Thomas, had moved from Wensleydale to Liverpool where he prospered as a merchant. John in fact had joined with him in partnership as linen drapers. Thomas progressed to privateer owning and banking. His second daughter, Alice, married Sitwell Sitwell in 1791, and was the great-great-grandmother of Osbert, Edith and Sacheverell Sitwell. Alice died in 1797, a month after giving birth to a son.[7] Thomas's son, James (1782—1868), after a distinguished scholastic career was appointed a judge and was made Baron Wensleydale of Walton. In his will Ralph left legacies to two nieces and a sister, £10,000 for the maintenance of Thomas, and the rest of the considerable Parke property to James.[8]

Beldy Hill mine continued to be worked without interruption until the long story of mining in the dale ended about 1880. The hillsides of the Swale and Swinnergill bear witness to it, and Crackpot Hall itself in ruins adds to the desolation. Those who have farmed the land report no traces of houses near East Gill, but remains of the sod fence on the north side of Hall out-pasture are still visible.

A personal recollection links up with this account. In August 1932, 160 years after these events, we remember walking from Keld along the track to Crackpot Hall on the way to Swinnergill. As we passed below the remains of Beldy Hill mine, an absolute silence prevailed and no movement stirred, until farther on we saw a horse and a small family group raking hay on the sloping meadows elevated high above the Swale. We joined them — the farmer, his wife and a small daughter running about barefoot playing with a sheepdog puppy. Presently two boys came home from school and the afternoon drinkings were fetched.

The name of the family was Harker. The Harkers left Crackpot Hall and Metcalfes took their place. But in 1953 the house was declared unsafe. It was not easily reached by motor traffic, and its stonework and lintels had slipped owing to leadmining subsidence. Somehow it is a fitting end.

1   Based on three 'Memoranda of Beldy Hill Affairs' (diaries) kept by John Parke from 1769—1772 and one account book 1766—1770. MSS now lodged at the North Yorkshire County Records Office, Northallerton; 'Argument of Alexander Wedderburn Esq., his Majesty's Solicitor General in the Cause of Lord Pomfret against Smith' printed in 1773, now lodged at the North Yorkshire County Records Office, Northallerton; Depositions of witnesses in the Beldy Hill trials, MS lent by Mr J L Barker; NYCRO ZKU VI-12 Beldy Hill/Swinnergill, and ZLB 3/2 depositions of Thomas Smith, J Parke, J Scott and partners, 1768.
2   NYCRO Pub No 6, T R Hornshaw, *Copper Mining in Middleton Tyas*, 1965, for pedigree of the Hartleys of Middleton Tyas.
3   NYCRO Pub No 16, L P Wenham, *Richmond Burgage Houses in North Yorks, 1679—1820*.
4   A packhorse bell collar bought in 1941 at Leyburn, Wensleydale, when a private museum was sold can be seen at the Dales Countryside Museum at Hawes.
5   NYCRO ZLB 41/1-8. Two plans of Crackpot Hall farm and adjoining commons.
6   Letter from Thomas Smith to his agent Thomas Butson lent by Mr C Clarkson. This Thomas Smith had taken the name Smith.
7   *Liverpool Post* (4th April 1945), and Sir Osbert Sitwell, *Left Hand Right Hand!*, 1945, Vol 1, p 14.
8   Borthwick Institute, York. Will of Ralph Parke, 21st February 1809.

The Corn Miller

A thick leatherbound book, 42 cm long by 17 cm wide with 420 pages of entries, came into our hands in 1944 for one shilling and sixpence at the auction sale of the contents of a house formerly belonging to Hannah Terry (1855—1944) at Bainbridge in Wensleydale. Its boards are loose, cracked and rubbed, and the pages browned at the edges. But when George Terry, the corn miller of Bainbridge Mill, Hannah's great-grandfather, began to use it in February 1784 it would be a handsome volume.[1]

The miller himself realised its value, for at the foot of page four he wrote: 'George Terry Book/ Steal not this Book for fear of shame for hear you se the ownder name/ George Terry.' On the previous page he had begun to rule lines to make a narrow column on the left for the date, on the right three lines for columns for pounds, shillings and pence, leaving a wide space in the centre for the goods sold. At the end of the book the last entry for the sale of oatmeal is in 1818, and two pages of sales of cheese follow up to 1837.

George was the son of John Terry (1710—73), miller of Askrigg, a mile from Bainbridge, who had five sons and three daughters. The Terrys were one of the old families of Wensleydale — a Richard Tary lived at Bainbridge in 1301 and in the seventeenth century there were four distinct families of Terry. John, the Askrigg miller in the eighteenth century, had acquired considerable property and made a corner for his family in milling. The eldest son, Ralph, was miller at Coverdale, then Bellerby, then at Forcet near Richmond; John was miller at Redmire; James followed his father as miller at Askrigg; his daughter, Elizabeth, married Anthony Moore, miller at Horton-in-Ribblesdale; whilst George, the third son, as he records amidst the scribblings and blots on the inner board of the ledger, 'Entred of Baynbridg Mill the Twelft of June 1780'.

At that date, within a radius of eight miles of Bainbridge there were nine water corn mills, at Hawes, Askrigg, Nappa, Woodhall, Carperby, Redmire, Aysgarth, West Burton and Thoralby, all except Aysgarth on becks flowing into the River Ure and all competing for custom in the then well-populated dale. Bainbridge itself had two mills both on the River Bain, and George's, close to the bridge, was usually called Bainbridge Mill.

Bainbridge, Wensleydale. The mill can be seen in the centre with, in front of it, the mill garth, in which a house has been built.

Briefly, the mill, although on the west bank of the Bain in Bainbridge territory, appears to have been the medieval mill for the barony of Worton on the east bank. Until it was pulled down in this century, a building (then used as a stable), on the east bank near the bridge over the Bain, was described as the 'Old Kiln'.[2] Later a new mill was evidently built on the west bank, probably because the river was wearing away the site. This explains the two mills in one village.

In the seventeenth century the mill passed through various hands to Sir William Robinson (1655—1736) of Newby near York, from whom and his descendants, who were raised to the peerage as Barons Grantham, it was leased to Alexander and Emmanuel Fothergill and their undertenants. From 1745 to 1754 the mill was extensively repaired, even to the replacement of the water wheel. Mills and their watercourses were always in constant need of repair, and as we shall see the mill was rebuilt in 1797. George Terry does not record the rent or the landlord's name, but again as we shall see the mill remained in the hands of the Robinsons until 1859.

When George Terry took over, hardly any corn was grown in upper Wensleydale. Some needed for the mills for grinding came from the lower dale. Most was bought

Bainbridge prior to 1920. The three-storied Bainbridge Mill is seen in the centre on the west bank of the Bain, and the kiln/stable, now pulled down, is the one-storied building on the east bank close to the bridge.

in during Terry's early days at Richmond and later mostly at Leyburn markets. At first George kept six horses for transport, not only to fetch corn but to deliver meal daily, weekly and monthly to his customers. Most of them regularly bought oatmeal by the peck (quarter of a bushel), sometimes half a peck, or a hoop (a quarter of a peck), or a bowl (two bushels) or by the load (twenty-four pecks or six bushels). A peck of oatmeal weighed about a stone, or fourteen pounds. The day-to-day entries in the ledger confirm in detail that oatmeal (eaten as porridge, oatcake, hasty pudding, gruel and so on) was — as is often stated — the staple diet of the Yorkshire Dales.

The miller also sold wheatmeal (often by the hoop), malt, barley meal, flour, occasionally maslin (a mixture of wheat and rye), beans, pease, very occasionally blendings (a mixture of beans and pease) and sacks of seeds. Pease were eaten as porridge or pudding, but were also fed to horses, sheep and pigs. From time to time George also supplied his customers with a variety of goods: milk, butter, cheese, coals, apples, potatoes, bacon, hams, flannel and oil cake. He was shrewd and bargains were dear to his heart.

He allotted a page, sometimes two pages, sometimes half a page or less to each customer, with the name, place of residence and infrequently the occupation at the top. He prefixed the better-off with mister: Mr William Fothergill (Alexander's son) of Carr End near Semerwater, Mr John Pattison, exciseman of Askrigg, Mr Anthony

Bainbridge Mill, on the River Bain. The lower addition by the water enclosed the water wheel.

Wharton, master of Yorebridge Grammar School, Mr Woodhouse, workhouse master. The occupations give a conspectus of those flourishing at the time: attorney-at-law, shopkeeper, hosier, stockinger, tailor, joiner, clockmaker, post rider, cooper, glazier, slater, woolcomber, brewer, doctor, miner, collier, cobbler, shoemaker, blacksmith, butcher, gardener, and a 'Dansen Master' at Bainbridge. Nicknames only very occasionally appear, although they existed, if not as prevalent as in Swaledale.

Numerically his customers, judged by the ledger, varied from 41 in 1784, dropping to 20 and 30, rising to 37, the peak, in 1798 after the rebuilding of the mill, and gradually diminishing in the first decade of the nineteenth century to 10 in 1810 and 18 in 1813. Cash sales are not recorded. Some names recur throughout the book. But change did occur. From 1785 to 1793 his brother-in-law, Anthony Moore, was by far his best customer. He bought five, six and seven loads of oatmeal and wheatmeal at a time, and for instance from March to November 1786 bought meal worth £52 16s. Anthony bought sacking and harden for pokes, and was charged carriage, which was unusual. On the other hand the Rev Anthony Wharton, master of the grammar school from 1794, was then a new customer. At first he regularly bought the normal pecks of oatmeal, but by 1805 he had begun to take in boarders and was buying oatmeal by the half load. In 1811 his Christmas dinner, a 'gouse', cost him five shillings and threepence.

The following, the account of the dancing master, Richard Lawson, in 1791, may be taken as a sample of a small order:

June 1	2 pecks of oatmeal	3	4
	Do peck of Wheat Meal	1	5
4	hupe of flower		6
11	peck of oat meal	1	7
28	2 peck of oat meal	3	2
30	Do half peck of flower		10
June 30	half peck flower		10
July 3	peck of wheat meal	1	4
4	peck of wheat meal	1	4
6	peck of oatmeal	1	7
18	left unpayed		6
August 10	2 pecks of oat meal	3	2
	half a peck of wheat (sic)		8½
15	2 pecks of oatmeal	3	2
17	half peck of wheat meal		8½
19	half peck of wheat meal		8½
20	peck of wheat meal	1	4
24	peck of wheat meal	1	4
	Lefte unpayed		2

Many of the accounts are complicated by the endemic borrowing. Both his customers and occasionally Terry himself borrowed small sums. Annual, six-monthly or monthly payments were usual, and at times odd sums were brought forward and debts paid in instalments of as little as sixpence a time. Accounting was chaotic. When a transaction was finished, George generally crossed off the whole or part page.

As an example of the scarcity of money, take the case of George Danial, gardener to John Pratt of Askrigg, racehorse owner, who employed a comparatively large staff. From June to December 1784, Danial bought coals, in all eleven loads at one shilling and fourpence a load, and eight pecks of coals at a shilling. By the end of November he had paid off half and, still owing eight shillings, he began paying off in sixpences and shillings, and once threepence. In all there were seven instalments, and these were not cleared until the 3rd April 1785.

Or consider William Terry's accounts. William was a glazier and probably a relation. For a start, £1 is brought forward from a previous account, and beginning on the 17th October 1784, William buys pecks of oatmeal and wheatmeal. On the 20th October, George 'Lente to William wife 2s. 0d.', and again on the 1st March 1785 'Lente to wife 5s.'. On the 16th April, 'Layd downe for 3 oringes 4½d.' and 'Layd downe for a Bed Tiken 7s.' is entered. On the 22nd May, when he lends William himself 5s 6d, he received £1 10s in cash and, balancing up the accounts, found that £1 10s 6½d was due to him. The entries continue, and one on the 13th July further confounds the issue: 'Lente to George Lee one guiney and I was to take it of[f] William Terry'. In 1784 the account with James Dinsdale, butcher, of Newbiggin near Askrigg, includes sales of pecks of oatmeal, loans 'Lente in Bras to James Dinsdale 12s. 8d.', and the purchase of a leg of mutton 8lb in weight for 2s 8d.

Whilst obviously supplying the immediate vicinity of Bainbridge, the range of his customers extended from Stalling Busk up to Raydale House beyond Semerwater, to farmhouses on the north side of Wensleydale (Abbotside) from Skell Gill to Camshouse to Shaw Cote, to Askrigg where he had customers in spite of the mill there and at Nappa nearby. He supplied oatmeal once to Angram in upper Swaledale and twice to Oxnop and Gunnerside in that dale, in the latter two cases probably to a relation and an old customer, James Tiplady.

Whilst he had rounds, those near at hand may well have fetched their meal. Some buy frequently, such as Mr Woodhouse, the workhouse master at Bainbridge, who buys two pecks of oatmeal and small quantities of other meal more often than weekly, for instance on nine days in the months of July and August 1788.

A customer, James Davey, moved from Low Foss on Raydaleside in February 1785 to Sargill Parks, to a remote house, Park Hall, now gone, beyond Skell Gill on the moors of Abbotside. Davey took the precaution of buying oatmeal by the load and often bought ten, even twenty pecks at a time. He once bought a pig for twelve shillings and is supplied with a ten pound cheese for three shillings and fourpence. One customer on Abbotside lived at Hole House, now a lost hamlet. James Metcalfe of Raydale House was another distant customer who bought large quantities at once, especially in winter.

Oatmeal kept if it was packed tight to exclude air. Within recollection, a meal ark (large chest) was part of the equipment of a Dales kitchen, and the meal was trampled down in it — at Starbotton in Wharfedale by a farm man wearing white socks.[4] Small quantities were packed in large crocks.

According to the entries in the ledger, there were two blacksmiths at Askrigg, and six at Bainbridge in the period covered — James Scarr, George Metcalfe, George Fawcett, James Dinsdale, Joss Smith and John Thompson. Competition for custom was keen so that George made advantageous bargains for shoeing. The first to be mentioned, George Lee, was employed on a daily basis to shoe horses for a year from November 1784. During that time there are eighty-four entries for shoeing, many for new shoes and others for 'removes' — old shoes re-used. For this frequent

A typical page from the miller's ledger. It records pecks of oatmeal, flour and wheatmeal bought by George Lee, blacksmith, in 1784.

attention the total cost was £4 14s 4½d. Lee was then dropped in favour of James Dinsdale, with whom George struck a bargain in December 1785. 'Begun with James Dinsdale Blacksmith to Shou 6 horses at the prise of 10 Shillings one horse pr year.' On the page of entries are mixed up with sales of oatmeal, twenty for shoeing horses sometimes named or described as Jock, the black horse, the old mare, the stag and 'Brufhilgalow' (Brough Hill Galloway). He sells James a *leay* (scythe) for 4s 6d and pays 3s 6d for a reckan (hook for a kettle) and a pair of hames (part of a horse collar). In 1788 the price per horse increased to 12s, but 'if aney Shoues be Loste the sade James Dinsdale is to pay for them'. He then returned to George Lee, followed by a contract with Joss Smith, and in 1796 one for 14s 6d a horse with James Sagar who was dismissed cursorily after less than two months: 'We gave over Shouen with Sager'.

So it went on. A contract with John Thompson in 1807 for two horses for a year at 16s 6d a horse included sharpening picks and chisels (for dressing millstones). But in November 1808 he is paying George Fawcett on a daily basis including repair work done to a kettle, a corn barrow and a *stee* (ladder), in all twenty-eight entries adding up to 16s. How poorly the craftsmen were paid!

Nor did men servants fare any

better. George hired men for the winter when there was more work, for haytime and sometimes for the year. In November 1802 he hired Adam Proctor for a year giving him a shillings as *earles* (earnest money) and three shillings a week. On the 5th January he noted that Adam was '2 Dayes of[f] at his father berer [burying]'. Next, James Miller was hired at the same rate.

In 1804 James Wedrald came for haytime and was given 2s 6d *earles* and for a month and two days offered £4 9s. During this time he was lent £1 15s, sold oatmeal and '2 penewath of eges' so that he was paid £3 0s 10d at the end. Wages rose, for when William Fuler was hired for twenty-nine weeks he was offered 5s a week. It was noted during that time that he had a day off at the sheep fair (Askrigg Hill Fair), another on Redmire Moor 'a volunteerin' (exercises with the Loyal Dales Volunteers), and had broken a shovel. Tenpence was twice deducted for the two days off and 1s 6d for the shovel. These, together with loans, reduced his final payment to £3 7s. It was usual to 'sub' for current expenses, and George was in line there with the practices of the times. How James Miller fared, who was off work in January 1804 for twenty days, we are not told. Sickness benefit was a long way away.

On the 20th June 1797 the familiar humming sounds of the mill and the booming of the water wheel ceased. On that day we read: 'George Terry Lefte over grinden at the owld mill at Baynbridge.' The building cannot have been large, because next day it was taken down by Thomas Metcalfe of Gunnerside, and four days later the ground works of the new mill were laid.[5] On the 9th September the roof was raised and George spent £1 on the rearing ceremony. Then, the millwright, John Sayre (sic) of Middleham, came into action. He employed two, three and four men almost daily including Sundays from the 24th October through November to the 22nd December. George Terry provided their meals, mostly three a day at fourpence each. (Sayre himself was given a meal or two for a shilling each.) When towards the end of December there was a rush on to finish the job, four men were sometimes given four meals a day. The total of 358 meals cost Sayre £6 5s.

In October the millwright put in the cog wheel and axle-tree, and in November part of the water trough. John Terry glazed the mill windows for £3, and in early December Peter Hutchinson 'Putt Joists and Dormon [beams] Runde the Mill and Barganed for Do £9 9s.', and later painted sash windows and doors. At length George wrote on the 18th December, 'the Blue Stones were sett to grinden'. Blue stones were of Dutch or German origin and were then used for grinding wheat.[6] On that day he ground twenty-six bushels, recorded in a special list headed 'An Account of the Wheat ground at the Mill by Me'. Up to the end of February, when the list ends, over 200 bushels had been ground.

On the 12th and 23rd January two new grey stones came from Addingham, forty miles south in gritstone country, and at the same time 'a new machine [for dressing wheat]'. On the 5th February 'the grey Stones were set to grinden and the Silender [for sifting] at the Same Time'. Thus two pairs of stones, the usual complement of a small mill, were installed. Unfortunately we are not given details of the total cost. George had been paid £190 twice by agents of the Robinsons. It was and is a small three-storeyed mill, 54 feet by 31 feet, superbly built of massive square-dressed stones with huge sills and lintels, still to be seen by the bridge at Bainbridge. The water wheel was 18 feet in diameter and 4 feet wide.

After only about seven months the new mill was fully in action. It had been a difficult time, and George had taken corn to be dried and ground at his brother James's mill at Askrigg, and had bought some meal from John at Redmire and Ralph at Coverdale. Never wasting an opportunity, he had meanwhile sold John a peck of apples for 1s 6d, 8¾lb of mutton for 3s 3d, and a new scuttle for 1s.

But now with improvement, business boomed. That year as many as sixty-seven customers came, mostly for the usual single pecks of oatmeal. In June 1798, William Thompson of Bainbridge bought pecks on thirteen days. Alexander Thompson of Grange began to buy an occasional stone of flour for 2s 8d. Thomas Woodert, corn factor of Askrigg, arrived more often than weekly with loads of wheat to be ground and dressed, and bushels of oats to be dried and ground. Both the old and the new mill had kilns, never mentioned in the ledger, and what fuel was used is not clear.

From 1785 to 1799, pecks of oatmeal rose in price from 1s 4d, varying slightly on the way to 1s 10d and 2s, rising to a peak of 5s and 4s in 1800 and 1801. Falling back to 1s 9d in the early nineteenth century, the price settled down to 2s 2d or 2s 3d up to 1815, rising again to 3s 6d a peck in 1818 when the accounts of oatmeal end.

It was of course the troubled period of the Napoleonic Wars and also years of several bad harvests. The rise had an effect. Farmers began to buy corn themselves from badgers (corn dealers) or at markets, and brought it to the mill to be ground. The trend started off in a minor way in 1795 and escalated. The practice was to take corn weekly to the mill and at the same time to bring back the oatmeal ground from the previous week's delivery. Oats were dried in the kiln and put through the stones twice, once for *shilling* (removing the husks) and once to grind it fine.

James Metcalfe of Askrigg, baker, naturally bought corn to be ground in quantity. From May to June 1797 before the mill stopped grinding he had 37½ loads of wheat ground at 1s 4d a load and eighty-four bushels of oats dried and ground at 1s 8d a bushel. He began taking corn again on the 11th February 1798, and up to the end of June had 104 loads of wheat ground and 414 bushels of oats dried and ground. James continued in this manner to the end of 1798. The total owing to the miller for the year was £15 15s 2d, a comparatively large sum.

A regular customer on the new lines was Thomas Parkin of Worton, who brought mostly wheat — sometimes weekly, sometimes less — often to be dressed and ground at 4½d a bushel. Thomas Fawcett, another customer won over to the new system, brought oats weekly to be dried and ground at 2d a bushel. For instance he took 186 bushels of oats and 18 bushels of wheat to be ground at the mill. George no doubt exacted multure as was usual for grinding. Once or twice he wrote 'no muter'.

At the same time, and to the end of the ledger, other customers continue to buy oatmeal by the peck, but wheatmeal as such had gradually faded out in 1804. (No doubt it had been coarse stuff, making heavy, unpalatable bread.) It was replaced by flour allied with a further change, first noted in the ledger on the 9th October 1796 when Robert Deves (Davis) of Raydale House bought 7 st 3 lb of flour for 13s. (Flour rose to 4s 8d a stone in 1810.) Pecks and bushels, the old dry measure, were on the way out, but as long as the ledger continues, stones and pounds, mass weight, were reserved only for flour.

More flour was being bought. Some, such as Thomas Wedrald, stuck to oatmeal. In 1813-14 he bought 48 pecks of oatmeal as against 5¾ stones of flour. On the other hand George Scarr, a long-standing customer, from buying oatmeal only in 1796 began in 1805 to buy small quantities of flour, until in 1812 he bought only 20 of oatmeal and 14¾ stones of flour, usually half a stone at a time.

Prices seem infinitely small. Ham and mutton cost 4d, and cheese 6d and 9d a pound. He sold '3 Moudy Warpe trapes' for 4½d. He also charged George Scarr 2d for catching a 'mowede warp [mole],' and once lent him 1d for a 'Beesam'. He sold a pig weighing 21 st 11 lb at 4s 7d a stone, and '1 talow loafe 2 st. 8 Ib. for 18s.'. This was a lump or cake of tallow required by chandlers. Oil cake at 1s or 1s 1d a stone was first sold in 1790. He himself bought goods — '2 Stones Soape' for 4d, and butter from Sally Pratt at from 9d to 10d a pound.

Once in 1791 he carted three iron ovens from Hawes to Aysgarth and Askrigg for James Lawson, a mason, and once a firkin of salt and candles for Thomas Whitton. But what were the six round bells and an iron 'boak' (balk) bought in 1791 from William Terry at 8d apiece. Packhorse bells? Once or twice he sold 'a pad'. People probably carried meal away balanced on pads on their heads, as recollected in Swaledale in the early 1930s. Very infrequently he records buying coal — in 1793 from West Pits on Abbotside carted by his brother Ralph, and in 1802 fifty-five and in 1804 fifty-six loads from Richard Mason and partners, who worked a seam on Blackstone Edge high on Askrigg Moor.

As was usual with millers, George ran a small farm and dealt in stock. Limited by shortage of land, this nonetheless provided additional income. To keep stock he had the Mill Garth, and had consistently over the years bought cattle gates in Askrigg and other cow pastures and some fields in Askrigg township.[7] But he also bought hay in at 6d a stone. In a transaction in 1793 he wrote: 'The full Weight of hay that I had from Shaw is 269 stones al Butt 3 pounds. Thare is the Ropes to take off this.' He also bought chaldrons of lime. Another winter he bought 238 stones of hay at intervals from John Thwaite of Mossdale, eight miles up the dale from Bainbridge. At sales he bid for hay and eatage if a farmer were leaving, as at Lease House above Askrigg, where he kept seven beasts in Slape Wath barn one winter. Lease House was eventually bought by the Terrys. The family in general coveted land and property.

As people took to fetching their own corn or as he employed someone to fetch it for him, the number of horses was reduced. But they were still a source of income. On the 1st June 1800 he wrote: 'We putt Mopsey to James Mason Stalyen,' and later 'Chestnut Stagg ditto' and 'Do the Lame mare'. On the 28th May 1808 he 'bargened wi parinton [Parrington] of Dente for 2 Mares putt to his hors for 15s. to be paid at seet [sight] of foals'. On the 10th August he sold a chestnut galloway for £14 14s to Thomas Coultherd of Worton. It was a long-drawn-out transaction. Thomas was still paying off in instalments in February of the next year, and, to add to the confusion, George borrowed the horse, paying 6s.

The mill accounts are interrupted by 'An Account of the Cows Buld this year', or in 1812 'Sould a Cow to John Robinson [Semerdale] at the prise of £16'. The first list of cows 'buld' appears in 1796, and two years later he has eight cows, described for instance as 'the Whi [heifer] we gott of Cobler Tom' or 'the mottled Whie with Swingin Back'. By 1809 he had a bull of his own and charged 2s 6d to serve other men's cows — twenty-four half crowns from the 7th January to the 10th June 1810.

The following January he sent Francis Milburn with a fat cow to Skipton. It was a three-day excursion and a thirty mile walk for man and cow, for which Milburn was paid 8s 6d. He cut short the distance by six miles by selling the cow *en route* at Cracoe for £25. It was a good price. In 1797 George had sold two fat beasts for £24 3s and three cows for £24, and in February 1788 he had bought a Scotch cow for £4 1s 10d. On 11 March 1806 he 'Sowld to Thomas Scarr our Bull Stirk at the prise of £6 6s. and was to have 3 cows Buld over and above'.

Similarly he dealt in sheep, monetarily some of the largest transactions in the ledger. In November 1790 he sold James Tiplady of Oxnop, Swaledale, 189 old sheep for £94 10s, eighty-four lambs for £25 4s, and a tar barrel for £1, and his brother, Edward, 190 sheep at 9s each. (Had he been to Middleham Moor Fair?) He sold a tup (ram) in 1803 for £1 6s 6d and usually noted when the tup was 'lowesed' in the late autumn. On the 26th October 1809 'the pet yow was Tupt with ower tup'. His own flock in the winter of 1807 was only thirteen Scotch lambs and twenty 'woold' sheep.

He kept a few geese and also dogs. Once he sold a load of dog meat, and in 1790 a 'Mastey Dog for 10s. 6d.' to Robert Sunter the elder of Carpley Green, a lonely farm on the moorland road leading to the Stake Pass to Wharfedale at 1,248 feet above sea level. (At the same time Robert bought 'one shilling meeshene [winnowing machine] for £7 and 90 bushels of Sinders for £2 12s. 6d.')

As long as he sticks to familiar items, his spelling suffices. But goose is always 'gouse' and guinea a 'guiney'. (Sometimes he is passed off with a 'light guinea', that is a clipped gold coin, the nuisance of the times). He makes himself understood with 'Oxanear' and 'bulakes' and on the 25th June 1803 he paid 4s for '8 Oweneses of Cheese Colouren'.[8]

From time to time, national and local events are recorded, interrupting the accounts in diary fashion. On the 24th May 1807 he wrote: 'Sett of[f] from Baynbridg to go to York upon Elexon and gave my voate to Mr Lashils [Lascelles] George Terry Baynbridg. Stayed 4 das.' It was of course the memorable election when many voted for another candidate, Wilberforce. In October 1802 he paid £1 1s to Clem Scarr for 'milisha' (a levy which could be made on people for a defence force). One year later his sons joined the Loyal Dales Volunteers. 'John & Ralph Terry Begun to Learn there Exercise and was Sworne to be trew to the King and Cuntrey as Loyal Subjexte at the Same Time But took no Bountey money as … Invasion was threatened by France. God Save King George the 3d and the Constutison.'

Foreign news evidently occasioned the joint purchase of a newspaper, the *Leeds Mercury*, for in 1799 he wrote, 'Poste Tomey Lefte the first Newspaper'. Post Tommy was Thomas Simpson of Askrigg, the post rider, who carried letters on horseback before the mail coach era.[9] On the 9th January 1808 he again wrote: 'The firste Newspaper Came to hand.' This was a weekly paper, not named and presumably for himself alone, bought from Thomas Baynes of Bainbridge.

In the early nineteenth century, the enclosure of several commons and cow pastures in which George had rights brought about the farming revolution. He records in detail the procedures. In 1806 the surveyor, Alexander Calvert of Richmond, measured Bainbridge pasture and stobbed it out. On the 11th May 1806 we read 'the payper of the Lottmentes and fences & how maney Akers What Sheep Gates I George Terry hath on Baynbridg fell 41 at 6d. Rente of my owne Do 31 at 2s. 6d. rente of Margrett Robinson of York'. George bought two gates in Bainbridge Side for £64 1s.

In July, Calvert measured Green Scar Mire, west of Bainbridge, and here George bought an allotment of nine acres one rood and twenty-two perches (where he sometimes kept his bull) for £247 16s. For each survey for measuring he paid Calvert in Bainbridge pasture £4 10s and similarly in Green Scar Mire £4 11s.

Following this the allotments had to be fenced with walls. George employed Jack Scarr and James Miller to build twenty-four roods at 3s 3d a rood and paid £5 8s 1½d. He bought a stone cart for 14s, 'forty-three Cartfuls of Throues [binding stones] from Hawes' for £1 5s 1d, and forty roods of stones at 5s a rood for £10. Stones had to be riven out of the ground, old walls led away, and some draining done. Throughout 1806 he employed other men in walling at 3s a rood. A new gate, loops and crooks cost him £1 5s. We see the face of the landscape changing.

To add to the turmoil, in some cases the enclosures were resented. On the 4th May 1807 Sander Milburn and his two sons 'pould Downe the fense & Drove his Beas throu the Lottment,' and again in July they 'Came in at Side gate without asen Leeve'. On the 12th April 1808 'Dockter Metcalfe [presumably finding his usual route blocked] wente ower Lottment with his horse and Threw ower gate of[f] the Croukes without Leve.' As late as 1811 others were threatening to throw down fences. (A note on the 5th September 1807 records 'a great flud of Water & Dele of Damige Don'.)

He also acted as agent for his landlord's family, for example Margaret Robinson of York, when fences were made in Cragdale, the Stake Pass, and in Water Ling pasture south of Carpley Green.

Although the tithe award for Bainbridge was not made until 1841, he recorded in 1803 a description of the payment of tithes. 'For Tithes to Be payd By pound Rentes for Everey Twenty Shilings Rente 2s payd oute of the Rentes. For Tithes of hay or grass in kind when mowen you are to knock it oute of Swath and then Every tenth Cock of grass is the Tyth men Due. For Tithes of Lambes you are to take as maney ones as you have 10 and then put your 9 Lambes be them Selves and then put one of your Beste Lambes to the 9 Lambes and then it makes 10 Lambes then you take 9 Lambes and the Tyth man takes one Lamb which makes 10.'

It appears that he was an overseer of the poor, and in 1809 recorded the first moves 'Concerning Building a Workhouse on Bowbrig hill Mr John Rider Wood the Leading Man'. Wood, a landowner, lived at Woodhall near Askrigg, and the suggested site at Bowbridge between Bainbridge and Askrigg was abandoned at a second meeting when 'mayjority of voates was for a Workhouse to be Builded at Baynbridge'. As it was. (Pease soup, incidentally, was workhouse fare in 1830.) He obtained money from the overseers of Constable Burton to be paid to Jane Blades called a 'penshun' — 2s a week under a settlement order.

He also organised the cutting of snow over three days in March 1804 when twenty-one men were employed, some for the day at 1s 9d and some for half a day at 9d. Cutting a smaller fall of snow the next winter cost 12s.

An interesting item in 1791 without the cost given was the building of a cheese press by James Lawson and his apprentice. Evidently in a separate building with door top and stone cheeks, it would be of the type with a huge stone weight. The new press brought several sales — Matthew Wedrald bought 97 lb of cheese for £1 2½d, and George Scarr 22½ lb for 4s 8½d.

By 1810 George's customers as recorded in the ledger had dwindled to ten, rising again to eighteen in 1813, but falling back to ten and finally seven in 1817. The miller was then seventy-six and at the end of that year he retired. A late entry in 1822/23 records sales of cheese at 60s a hundredweight sold to a Thomas Durham, in total £80. A page or two in another hand take the ledger up to 1837.

George died in 1824 and his sons did not carry on the mill. They both became farmers, one at Lease House and one branch eventually settling at Cravenholme, a farm close to Bainbridge. Alexander Chapman became miller and in his day a third pair of millstones, French Burr, were installed. After he died aged eighty in 1858 the mill was sold by auction the following year to Richard Cockbone by Thomas Philip Weddell, Earl de Grey, who was a Robinson who had changed his name to Weddell.[10] Cockbone, whose family had been millers at Hawes, also owned the Low Mill at Bainbridge. Bainbridge mill ceased to function as a corn mill, eventually becoming a saw mill and is now a joiner's shop. A water turbine has taken the place of the mill wheel and at the west end a house has been added since George Terry's day.[11]

All the other little water corn-mills, first one then another, were to cease to grind corn and with them went the life they had witnessed. Most of the occupations of the customers and many of the names recorded in the ledger have gone, even including the blacksmith. The focal point of the mill in village life vanished. The Terrys themselves have left the neighbourhood, although four great-great-grandsons of George live elsewhere. One branch, that of John Terry of Redmire Mill (taking barrels of gold sovereigns with them), emigrated and settled in Tasmania.[12]

Both mills at Bainbridge are still there. The Low Mill has been restored, but the interior of George Terry's mill has been cleared of milling machinery. However, several millstones remain, three sunk in the floor, and in the mill garth, one

George Terry, farmer of Cravenholme, the miller's grandson, drawn by E Forbes in Edmund Bogg's

which is incised with the evocative initials and date 'J S 1798'. George left nothing to remember him by except this remarkable ledger.

1   Based on the account book (1784-1837) of George Terry, corn miller of Bainbridge mill. MS in the authors' possession.

2   *Ripon and Richmond Chronicle*, 15th January 1859. Advertisement for the sale of Lot 1, a water corn-mill with the machinery at Bainbridge. Lot 2, all that building commonly called the 'Old Kiln' now used as a stable on the east side of the River Bain adjoining the main road. Information kindly given by Mr and Mrs David Hall who have also suggested the connection with Worton.

3   Leeds Archives Dept N H 1272 and 2187.

4   E Pontefract and M Hartley, *Wharfedale* (1938), p 66.

5   To avoid confusion it must be stated that these details given in A Raistrick's *Industrial Archaeology* (1972), p 236, do not apply to Low Mill, Bainbridge but to Terry's mill.

6   It is to be noted that Matthew Wadeson imported blue mill-stones to Stockton-on-Tees from Rotterdam in the early nineteenth century. They were 3 feet 8 inches in diameter and 11 inches deep.

7   Coleby Hall archives lent by Mr J Scarr. From 1772 to 1802, George Terry bought 8¾ cattle gates in Askrigg Cow Pasture, two in Sleddale south of Hawes, and closes in Askrigg township.

8   In the present day Annato, a vegetable dye, is used to stain cheese. It is added to the milk just before the rennet and does not affect the flavour. Information kindly given by Mr T C Calvert. Perhaps George Terry used colouring when his cheese was a poor colour.

9   Postboys or post riders were paid by the postmaster, probably that at Bedale, whence, in the late eighteenth century, posts were despatched three days a week to Askrigg. A riding post from Hawes to Dent was not discontinued until the 1840s.

10   Indenture of 1859 lent by the present owner of the mill, Mr T L Parrington.

11   Where George Terry lived is not known. A Chapman occupied Coupland, now Summerfield House, a detached house on the west side of Bainbridge green, then the property of the Robinsons.

12   See also G M Dow, *Samuel Terry* (1974). This concerns the Terry's who emigrated to Australia.

Yeomen Farmers

For more than three centuries a Garth lived at or near the hamlet of Crackpot on the south side of Swaledale. Situated in a deep cleft called Crackpot or Haverdale Gill, it lies on a narrow road, which past the last farmhouse at Summer Lodge, rises steeply as a rough track to cross the high moors to Wensleydale. Near this route is the cave or pot, Fairy Hole, which gives the hamlet its name.

Crackpot in the manor of Grinton had been part of the possessions of Bridlington Priory until the Dissolution of the Monasteries, and a Richard Garth first settled at Crackpot as a leasehold tenant in the early seventeenth century. Family tradition has it that he came from London, had married the daughter of one of the buyers of the manor of Grinton from Elizabeth I, and that the collection of pewter, still there

The Garths' house at Crackpot, dating from 1732.

The hamlet of Crackpot and Crackpot Gill, Swaledale. The Garths' house is by the dark tree.
Gunnerside is in the distance on the far left.

in the twentieth century, had been brought with them. Eventually a John or James built the house at Crackpot as witness the present dated doorhead IG 1722.

At the end of the eighteenth century, Francis Garth lived at Crackpot, whilst his brother, James, had Bank Heads, a farm on the road from the hamlet to Gunnerside Bridge. But James left for the south, and so one family remained in Swaledale, eventually adding Bank Heads to their properties. Beginning in 1795, members of three generations of this family kept journals or work memorandums as they called them, contained in six books. The first, Francis Garth (1732—1810), only briefly enters the picture. His son, Richard (1768—1848), kept two of the journals, and thereafter his son, a second Francis (1817—1911), kept four books, the last one continued after his death until 1936 by one of his two daughters, Mary Elizabeth Garth. The youngest daughter, Margaret Frances Garth (1879—1970), lent us the diaries and recollected old times. [1]

The diarists were men of standing, assuming positions of responsibility, playing a beneficial role in their lifetimes and leaving an imprint on mid-Swaledale visible to this day in walls, buildings and trees. They were involved in the many changes taking place: enclosures and the stinting of the pastures, tithe redemption, the formation of poor law unions, the establishment of a police force, the building of a church, chapels, schools, vicarages, houses, bridges and the fortunes of the leadmines. They employed a servant man and a servant girl who often lived in, and when necessary, especially in haytime, recruited other help which in the well-populated leadmining community — at any rate up to about 1880 — was readily available. Sometimes the school master or school mistress, who taught the school at Crackpot endowed by Ruth Garth (1733—1764) of Nettlebed House, half a mile away in Swaledale, also lived with them.

The entries are brief and factual, entirely concerned with the men's work. Sundays are ruled off and mostly left blank. Family births, deaths (always with the hour of the day given) and marriages merit importance by being recorded in a larger hand. Almost the only comments concern the weather, constantly mentioned, then as now the preoccupation of all who live in the Dales.

Yet, when the journals begin, Francis and his son Richard were, besides farmers, self-employed masons and to a lesser extent joiners, journeying all over upper Swaledale. They erected houses, bridges, cowsheds and walls, set kitchen ranges, ovens and boilers, put up tombstones, hung a grindstone, hewed cisterns, as well as working at leadmines and at Tan Hill coal pit on buildings, shafts, a water-wheel case, and at 'dialling' (surveying in mines) using a miner's compass. They went to Swinnergill, Dalehead and Bank Heads quarries for stone, and to Muker Edge, Harkerside, Stockdale above Thwaite, and elsewhere for stone slates. Sometimes they leased quarries. In 1801 Richard, who was one of ten partners at the mine, worked for weeks on end delivering and putting in wood at Lane End mine above Keld where the Birkdale and Sleddale becks meet to become the Swale.

'Walling' as an entry occurs regularly. In September 1795 they pulled down the old school house, presumably at Crackpot, and rebuilt it. The next year they built Stonesdale Bridge at the head of the dale on the road to Tan Hill. On the 22nd September 1798 they pulled down part of Nettlebed house (in one day according to the entry), rebuilt it, were putting in a fireplace on the 22nd October and finishing plastering on the 6th November. In March 1809 they 'set out the new chapel at Low Row'.

At this time, enclosures of pastures and commons had begun. South-west of Crackpot stretched a cow pasture of 429 acres, in which in proportion to their holdings they and others had cattlegates and horsegates. Across it ran the peat road leading on to the common at Sun Gate. In 1809, after a meeting at an inn at Reeth and the appointment of a commissioner, the pasture was enclosed by deed poll, and the Garths were awarded fifty-three acres.[2] So that year from April to September they were leading stones and walling that part of it called Sunside, a twenty-acre field, of which the high end alone measured 31 rood 1 yard long. This important

*Crackpot. The building in the centre with a chimney is the old school house, now pulled down.
The Garths' house is on the right.*

undertaking and improvement was matched in 1834 by the building of Crackpot
Moor fence (Bloody Wall) which took Richard, his two sons, the farm man and five
other men 151 days' work.[3]

In February 1801, Richard was canvassing for subscriptions for a bridge, probably of wood, to replace the Wood Bridge which crossed the Swale at Isles just
below Crackpot.[4] He drew a design and on the 30th October 1802 was 'setting up
bridge at Isles'. This was rebuilt in 1835 when a bottle with an inscription 'written
on parchment & sealed' in it, was put in the foundations of the north pier. The River
Swale is omnipresent throughout the journals. Stones are led from it, piles put in,
and hay was made on an island in it, not to mention the destruction caused by
'Great floods' continually being noted.

'Sawing at Gunnerside' (no doubt in a sawpit with a top and bottom sawyer)
occupies days, and once 'Turning naves' (hubs for wheels) is entered. On the 28th
June 1808 they were making a peat cart, and on the 23rd August 1809 'mending
Stone cart Wheel'. Timber for the leadmines, sought for as far afield as Stockton
and Craven, was supplied in quantity. In July 1802 they sold a piece of oak 13 feet
long and 18½ inches girth for use at the Old Gang mines, three miles away immediately across Swaledale from Crackpot.

Isles Bridge, Haverdale Mill and Crackpot Gill, lined with trees running up to the horizon, in 1883. Note the rebuilt arches of the bridge, brought down after one of the nineteenth century floods.

Aware of the acute shortage of timber, in 1802 the Garths began planting seedling ashes, elms, Scotch firs, larch and oaks, and nine years later they embarked on a major planting scheme, buying thousands of larch, hundreds of sycamore, birch, mountain ash, and fifty poplar. Planting continued on a lesser scale. Purchases included two Orleans plums for the well-cultivated garden, where gooseberry bushes, peas, beans, carrots and cabbages were grown. The plantations of larch at Bank Heads, Crackpot Gill, near the river and elsewhere were cared for and thinned, so that many years later when from time to time, for example in the First World War, they were sold, they provided a useful source of income.

After the first Francis's death and when Richard, having married Sarah Kearton of Thwaite in 1806, established a family, the picture changes. In that period enterprise was in the air, as witness the rise of the Knowles and Parke families of Swaledale based on trade — hosiery and leadmining. The basis of the Garth's prosperity was constant improvement and forward planning. Land was bought and stock increased. Farming, surveying, some interests in leadmining and coal pits continued, but building work now diminishes, eventually to cease altogether. As an example of progress, a plan of Bank Heads drawn by Richard in 1823 shows that between 1814 and 1817 a new cowhouse was built, another rebuilt, and three groups of trees were planted, two on steep banks and one on top of a 'Great Perpendicular Scar'. An entry in Richard's diary also records that a new house was built at Bank Heads in 1831.[5]

The major interest of the journals lies in the manifold activities, the long period covered, and the resultant picture of a self-contained former life and round of the seasons different from that pursued in the dales today.

Because of the high price of corn following the French Wars, the Garths cultivated a certain amount of arable land, where they grew oats, barley, wheat, potatoes, turnips and mangel wurzels. A four-acre flat field by the river, Burblet, belonging to Bank Heads, was ploughed in 1817. There were 13 acres of arable land on Crackpotside and 25 in Grinton and Harkerside.

For fuel they dug peat (25 loads in 1807), and continually fetched loads of coal for themselves and for other people from Tan Hill pit and to a lesser extent from William Gill in Arkengarthdale and Cotterdale pits in upper Wensleydale. They led limestone from different kilns for lime to dress the land, eventually building a kiln themselves. They cut and gathered *seaves* (rushes) for bedding, pulled *threaves* of ling for thatching buildings, and kept bees for honey for sweetening food. They must also have made cheese, but only a few references occur to taking it to villages.

In January and February, before snowstorms, they are gathering in the sheep, ploughing, leading out turnips, chopping firewood, pruning gooseberry bushes and trees; in March and April, 'Pairing' land and ploughing for potatoes, making land drains, sowing the garden, setting potatoes (usually with four or five helpers), spreading manure, sowing oats, fetching lime from the kiln, harrowing and rolling turnip land, examining ewes for lambing. In May and June, day by day they are getting peats, again with help (often women), scruffling the turnips, turning ewes and lambs on to the moor, taking swarms of bees. On the 19th June 1826, Richard had them 'nicely hived at 3 o'clock & not a Bee in the hive at bedtime'. Whitewashing the interior of the house later changed to paperhanging. In 1799 they bought a pig for £1 9s 6d at Askrigg June fair.

July and August found them clipping sheep, often still getting out and dressing (spreading) manure, working hay for a fortnight or for much longer according to the weather. In September they were cutting corn. In a poor time, haymaking overlapped with mowing oats, and once in 1838 because of 'a great wind' they were 'setting up wheat with stakes', leading bedding, thatching stacks, getting ling for kindling, and taking honey, sometimes four hives. The quantity of honey was considerable — in 1801, 8 st 2 lb from one hive.

In October the corn was harvested, potatoes taken up, more bedding led, and the sheep were salved to prevent disease. (This was a long and tedious operation, parting the wool and smearing each sheep with a mixture of tar and grease.) In 1845,

20 lb of tar and 25 lb of grease were bought. In November and December there was threshing, winnowing, cutting chaff (a chaff cutter was acquired in 1857), and taking corn to be ground at Gunnerside Mill, pulling turnips, sometimes killing and cutting up a bull and always one to five pigs. The cows were laid in the barns for winter and the tups loosed among the sheep. The entry for the 11th November 1816 recorded a sorry time: 'Getting in corn in Burblet, hard frost, streams in Swale floated with ice.' A few entries state that they are 'paring bulfronts' and sometimes leading them to the yard. Bulfronts or bulforeheads were big tufts of grass, so called from their resemblance to the tufty hair on a bull's forehead. Perhaps they were used for fuel.

Haymaking then as now was all important, and the numbers employed indicated the escalation of their farming activities, as well as the often feverish rush to beat the weather. In 1804 five men and two women were hired, some for the day, some for the week. In 1824 Richard first devoted a page of his journal to a tabulated hay-list with the names of the 'hayworking miners', as Miss Garth called them, at the top and dates down the side, a convenient device to record in columns the different number of days worked by each person. Sometimes a few came from Westmorland and Cumberland.

In 1837 when twenty-three names occur, Thomas Metcalfe — paid 2s 6d a day for mowing — earned £3 15s, much the largest sum . Peggy Metcalfe, working 10½ days, was paid 12s. For other work the men were paid at the rate of 1s 6d an hour and the women at 1s and often 6d. This of course included meals throughout the day. In 1845, 30 men and 5 women were hired. A crisis befell them in August 1848 when Richard's sister's child died of scarlatina, and the Garths at Crackpot went down with scarlet fever and had to let some of the meadows by the acre.

'Begun hay' generally appears about the 11th or 13th July, the traditional time for starting. But by the 1870s they are surprisingly beginning in June. In three consecutive years, 1824 to 1826, fine weather meant that they finished in a fortnight 'never having been put off work since we begun'. It was notable enough on the 24th July 1826 to enter 'not a Cloud all day'. On the contrary in 1839, delayed by bad weather, haymaking started on the 26th July and finished on the 23rd September, because 'through the season almost constant heavy Rain scarcely any hay got but laid out 2 or three weeks'.

On the 11th July 1862 there appeared an important entry: 'At Askrigg Fair Bought one of Woods Patent Mowers of Mr Bushby of Newton-le-Willows for £20.' (This machine is remembered rusting and disused in a barn.) Three days later they were 'mowing in Burblet' which in May had been sown with rye grass and clover seeds. But the number of helpers does not diminish significantly, and ten years later there were eighteen helpers. In June 1875 a haymaker was bought at Richmond, and in 1889 a new mowing machine was again bought at Askrigg. Francis Garth was anxious to give employment in hard times, but he foresaw that as the leadmining industry failed,

The old and the new. Scythemen and an early mowing machine at Muker about the turn of the century.

hiring staff would become more and more difficult. He bought further machines to replace the scythes and rakes — a move deeply resented by the helpers.

Miss Garth remembered that in haytime they used to bake ten stone of flour a week, and when taking out the drinkings they packed the food in two laundry baskets fitted on panniers on each side of a pony. At the end of haytime it was the custom for all to sing hymns outside the windows, usually Methodist hymns like 'When shall we all meet again/We shall meet on that beautiful shore' — a hymn which brings a lump into the throat. In those days, when people went to chapel they used to stand outside singing hymns before going in. The building was small and it was a case of who could get in.

Entries concerning stock occur much less often, except those for 'cows bulled' and 'cows calved'. At the back of one book beginning in 1819, Richard keeps a record of cows and calves often sold, and at the back of another Francis lists the sums paid from 1854 to 1870, at first 3s and later £1, for other men's cows served by

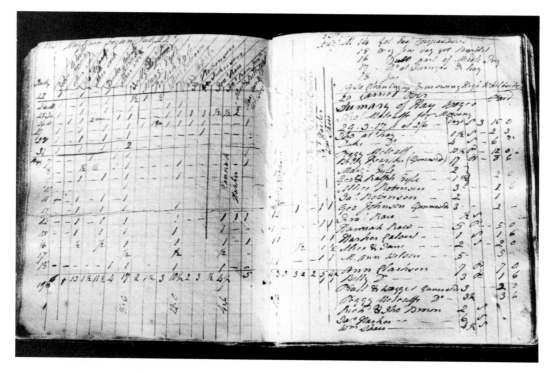

Pages from the Garth diaries, showing a haytime list on the left and the wages paid on the right.

a bull. Many paid nothing at all. As time went on, the Garth's effort to persuade people to improve their stock was noticeable in the much better beasts seen grazing on the roadsides and on the smallholdings of the miners.

In the late 1850s and early 1860s, Francis began to establish a herd of pedigree Shorthorns, a breed originating in the late eighteenth century on the borders of Yorkshire and Durham, and he attended sales of well-known breeders: Mr Jacques's, Mr Wetherall's, Mr Jolly's at Warlaby near Northallerton. In 1856 he bought a bull stirk, Sunbeam, for £30 at Darlington. Horace, a white bull, came from Mr Jolly's herd and another bull from that of Thomas Willis at Carperby in Wensleydale. Bumper, a red bull bought in 1863 from Mr R Thornton of Stapleton near Darlington, appears most frequently in the pedigrees.

He first entered three cows bred at Crackpot in *Coates's Herd Book for Short-Horned Cattle* in 1869, and four years later listed eleven bulls, three already sold. Even eight of these massive animals grazing on the pastures must have been a sight. When in 1875 he and others joined together to form the Shorthorn Society, the herd books were continued. In those years he records selling twenty-three head of cattle to other breeders, and he sent one of his pedigree cows, Annetta Windsor, to be served by a bull from the herd belonging to R S Bruere at Braithwaite Hall in lower Wensleydale, at least twenty-five miles away. Unlike the Willises, whose beasts won many prizes at shows far afield, Francis eschewed competition.[6]

Nevertheless, fat-stock shows and the new agricultural exhibitions being promoted were often attended. In July 1848, Francis had gone to York for the Royal Agricultural Society's meeting, and in August 1862 he visited York again for that of the Yorkshire Agricultural Society. By now not all the stock was supported on the farm. In April 1856, fourteen stirks and heifers were driven to Widdale above Hawes to eat hay, and he had gates (rights) on Askrigg pasture.

When a bull was killed in November 1856 it weighed 69 st 3 lb and the hide 8 st 12 lb. The animal was cut up and pickled for winter meat. Some meat was sold. In July 1841, six cattle in the home pasture were affected by the rinderpest, then rife; in June 1852 a red and white *why* (heifer) was struck and killed by lightning (a not unknown occurrence) in Birks Allotment, and on the 4th October 1892 'Bull Marshal [was] found dead in his stall'. Here Francis's skill and knowledge gained from the vetinerary books he owned had failed, but neighbours often turned to him for help.

ROSE OF LUCKNOW at 6 YEARS OLD,
Bred by Mr T. Willis, Manor House, Carperby near Bedale.

A typical pedigree shorthorn cow. This one, Rose of Lucknow, bred by Thomas Willis of Carperby, Wensleydale, won many prizes and is pictured in Coates's Herd Book, *vol 18, 1869.*

Cattle rather than sheep predominated on the farm, and so sheep in the mid-nineteenth century numbered only 195, including 3 tups. About half were blackfaced and half hornless Mug sheep (Wensleydales). In 1833 Richard bought four Mug ewes costing £7 2s and a Mug tup for £1 17s. On the 28th March four years later, five Mugs lambed eleven lambs. By 1875 his son, Francis, with more grassland available, had increased the flock to 214. In 1857 salving, a practice which Francis had always disliked, was discontinued and dipping instituted. It is remembered that a woman, Duke Mary, who lived on Whitaside, shepherded Francis's sheep.

The number of horses kept is not recorded, but apart from their use they were part of the economy of the farm. Year by year a mare (in 1803 one was bought at Boroughbridge Fair) had a foal; and sadly in 1823 a foal broke its leg. On the 6th October 1838 they were seeking a Galloway, supposing it stolen; in 1855, selling a filly at Brough Hill fair for £20; and in March 1878 old Jinny, aged nearly thirty, died. Another old grey horse called Captain, aged twenty-five, on the 21st December 1861 had to be shot because the teeth of its lower jaw were worn level with the gums and it could not support itself, and it was buried in the slack in High Pasture Bottom, .

By 1857 they acquired a gig, and a good deal later a large governess cart. When horses and carts were sent to Tan Hill it was twelve miles away. Long distances undertaken on horseback meant nothing to them. For instance, after finishing hay on the 8th September 1817, Richard the next day was at Tan Hill, on the 10th at Cotterdale, on the 12th at Reeth, and on the 15th at Brough near Kirkby Stephen in Westmorland. Places far afield involved absences of one or more days. 'At home' or 'About home' occurs regularly in the journals, recording the fact that they were not away.

Fairs were obligatory for the sale and purchase of stock. Those at Thwaite, Muker, Gunnerside, Reeth and Richmond (all in Swaledale) flourished and were attended. They always went to the annual fairs at Askrigg, including the July Hill Fair, to Hawes and Brough Hill in the early autumn, and sometimes to Leyburn and Middleham Moor in November. Occasionally they went as far as Northallerton, Darlington, Masham and Boroughbridge fairs, and in 1836 their servant man attended Stagshaw Bank Fair in Northumberland.

Just as a major change in the farming pattern occurred after the Second World War when tractors replaced horses, the 1860s proved to be a watershed at Crackpot. Some of the changes were consequent on the arrival of the railway at Richmond in 1846 and at Askrigg a little later in 1877. As we have seen they had ceased to salve sheep, and the first mowing machine was bought. Thenceforward the arable land was laid down to grass, and in the 1860s 'Men levelling' and 'Levelling ridges' is a frequent entry. Francis, then in his fifties, was building up his Shorthorn herd.

It is known that, whilst levelling the ground in Burblet, a Roman pig of lead was found. It was actually on the roadside, because the road formerly ran alongside this field on the west side of Haverdale Beck. Altered after the rebuilding of the bridge, it now runs on the east side. Was it part of a load being transported from Hurst to the Roman fort at Bainbridge? Unfortunately, as Miss Garth said, her father was a practical man, and he had it melted down to use for sealing iron crooks in stone gateposts.

Linseed cake, coals, Indian corn and potatoes are now fetched from Richmond fifteen miles away and later from Askrigg via six steep miles. Obviously it was cheaper to buy than to grow. In 1855 guano is being laid on Sunside. At the same time, work at the limekiln, from lighting it on the 1st June to leading twenty cart-loads of lime at the end of the month, was a time-consuming operation not yet abandoned. Bees were still kept with brief and very infrequent entries about them.

Throughout the journals, little is said about Haverdale Mill, built by Edmund Knowles in the early years of the last century, on the beck below the hamlet of Crackpot, for spinning yarn for knitting and for weaving carpets. Perhaps so large an industrial enterprise was regarded as an intrusion . They had, we are told, a very good carpet made there. On the 10th December 1836 we read that 'Mr Knowles first got water to the new Mill Wheel', and in 1851 'At the Sale of Mr Knowles Mill Machinery' when Francis bought a winch, and in 1904 'Sale of Site and ruins of

Haverdale House when the Garths lived there.

Haverdale Mill'. After the textile era it had become a corn mill, from which the Garths fetched meal with a donkey.

Nor is leadmining greatly in evidence, although both Richard and Francis benefited from shares in the mines and also in Tan Hill coal pit. On the 15th July 1802 Richard was drawing a plan of Whitaside mine and the next day he went to view the mining works of a new company, Easterby Hall, in Arkengarthdale. In 1811 he 'Went with Simon Harker to Nidderdale to canvise for Petitions to Parliament for rateing Duty Lead'. In 1861 they were leading wood and rails to Crackpot moor mine, a small mine just through Sun Gate. One of the few comments reads: '1830 marked throughout with the greatest distress in Swaledale which the oldest can remember. The exhausted state of the Mines the very low price of Lead & a Monopoly of the mineing concerns has reduced Wages to a Starving state — great numbers has with their families gone off & Pauperism become more general.' This was, however, only the beginning of the end.

Later, Francis is attending Whitaside Pay and the weighing of lead at Grinton smelt mill, and from early days he dialled at both lead and coal mines and once at Burtersett quarries in Wensleydale. On a lighter note on the 27th November 1866 he was 'At a Tea Meeting at the Old Gang Mines', an event promoted to celebrate the temporary improving condition of the mines. Tea began at noon. Rustic amusements followed, and two brass bands added 'their enlivening strains to the entertainment'.

From the windows of Haverdale House, to which the family moved in 1884, the two Miss Garths used to see the miners in their dirty clothes covered with yellow mud going and coming home from work along miners' trods. Miss Garth also remembered the pigs of lead heaped up at the corners of roads waiting to be carted away. Then, there were two or three families in all the small cottages. Sadly all of them fell empty. As the exodus swept on, Francis at first gave each family £5 to help them on their way, but so many were leaving that he had to reduce it to £3 and then £2.

As boys, he and his elder brother, Richard, had been educated first at the school at Crackpot, then as boarders at the anciently-founded grammar school at Kirkby Hill, north-west of Richmond. Richard took up the career of surveyor at a time when enclosures created urgent demand for maps and plans, and working in Dent, Grisedale, upper Swaledale and elsewhere he was made a commissioner. But marrying and settling at Hawes in Wensleydale, he died aged thirty-eight in 1853.

Francis himself was supposed to have consumption as a boy, but he resisted coddling, threw the windows wide open, got up at 5 am, never over-ate and grew strong, living as we have seen to be ninety-four. On the 13th June 1865, when he was forty-eight, he and Mary Clarke of Thwaite were married at Melbecks Church and went to Edinburgh for their honeymoon. Edinburgh had become familiar because Francis's cousin, Richard Lowther, had been educated there. Francis had two Garth aunts

Francis Garth of Crackpot, 1817—1911.

(his father's sisters), both of whom married parsons. In 1831, Eleanor had married the Rev John Metcalfe, a large landowner of Ings House, Hawes, and in 1845 Sarah had married the Rev Richard Lowther, a much-loved vicar of Muker. Although Sarah died young, Francis often saw the Lowthers, and the Metcalfe connection proved important.

In their early married life Francis and Mary Garth suffered grievous losses. Their first two daughters died in infancy, and their only son, Richard, in his second term at a boarding school, the new North Eastern County School, at Barnard Castle, caught a chill after running in a paper chase, contracted pneumonia and died at the age of sixteen. Two more daughters, Mary Elizabeth and Margaret Frances, were born in the 1870s, neither of whom married.

For many years, until the Rev John Metcalfe's death in 1873 and the settling of the will, Francis acted as agent for the Metcalfe's Wensleydale estates. He was instrumental in planting trees, and erecting houses, for example Yorescot near Bainbridge, Ashes near Hawes and Riggs House above Hawes. He negotiated on the Metcalfe's behalf with the railway companies for land both for the Settle-Carlisle and the Northallerton-Hawes lines. These occupations constantly took him to Wensleydale, and for years his family spent Christmas at Ings House.

The Garths were public-spirited, politically minded, and had a bent for science and drawing. The first Francis began to take the *York Herald* in 1801, and Richard took his family to lectures on thunder, volcanoes, astronomy and chemistry at Reeth and Richmond. He also started a book club at Muker with books of poetry, travel and history predominating. At the famous general election at York in May 1807, he voted for Wilberforce and Lascelles. He was present at Richmond at a meeting about the Reform Bill with 'Dinner in Market Place for about 1000 and near 100 flags with appropriate devices'. Later that year in December and in January 1835 he travelled with friends to Askrigg where the polls were held, and voted first for the Whig candidate, E T Cayley, and then for Duncombe and Cayley.

On the 24th August 1803, during the alarms of the Napoleonic Wars, Richard 'Went to Colne [in Lancashire] to hire a substitute for Ralph Harker in the Army of Reserve', and in November, December and January of the next year, having joined the Reeth and Muker company of the Loyal Dales Volunteers, he attended numerous parades, one 'with Gun and Accouterments' and at another 'fired with ball' for the first time. Other national events referred to are on the 21st March 1832, 'General fast day on act. of Cholera Morbus', and on the 7th October 1857, 'Day of fasting and Humiliation for the Indian Revolt by Royal Proclamation' (the Indian Mutiny).

In 1813 meetings were held, with Richard in the chair, with a view to incorporating Grinton with Bainbridge Workhouse, which was in Wensleydale, under Gilbert's Act (a poor law which allowed parishes to unite), but an entry in 1827 states 'At Grinton when Resolved to give up Poor house at Bainbridge', and in 1837 'joining

Grinton with Richmond Union of 46 parishes'. On the 7th February 1840 he was 'At a meeting at Reeth to Petition the Magistrates against a Police Force being established in the North Riding'. Resistance to change was built-in in the independent dales communities.

Although they attended chapel services, both Richard and Francis were devoted churchmen, so that the following entry is written by Richard in a large hand: '3 August 1841 at the Consecration of the Trinity Church Feetham [Melbecks Church] by the Rt Rev Charles Thomas Bishop of Ripon who Preached from the 122nd Psalm & 1st verse.' He himself had collected subscriptions towards the building of the church and the family then worshipped there. Muker and Melbecks vicarages, Muker and Gunnerside schools, and the chapel at Low Row (built in the nineteenth century) all benefited from the Garth's knowledge of building. On the 17th June 1851 Francis was 'At Richmond at the Visitation [archdeacon's] & went forward to London to the Great Exhibition of the Industry of all Nations held in Hyde Park.'

As usual in a closely-knit community, funerals were attended and mourners bidden. A person with a modest estate dies, the funeral follows, there is a sale of furniture, Francis values the hay, attends the sale of cattle and hay, and in about a fortnight takes the will to be proved. The Butsons, Birkbecks, Brodericks and Clarkes are family friends. On the 5th May 1820 it was 'Miss Birkbeck Birthday had about 20 of her friends to tea and supper', and on the 24th December 1885 'Had Lowrow & Gunnerside Brass Band to Supper'.

Their farming activities and public commitments left time for a few family outings and holidays. In the 1820s Richard took the children to Reeth Fair, and on the 19th May 1830 he was 'At Lane End Mine to See the Engine with Daughters'. This was a small steam engine recently installed. Later in Francis's day, visitors were escorted to view Kisdon Force near Keld. On the 27th June 1814 Richard set off to London, returning on the 8th July, but he does not reveal the reason for his visit. The first major holiday was taken at the end of May 1822 when the family was away for a few days at Newcastle and elsewhere. In September 1833 they went for ten days to Croft Spa near Darlington.

In June 1854 Francis visited Edinburgh with his sister and her family, and in June two years later he set out on an ambitious tour of Scotland, travelling as far north as Fort William, sailing down the Caledonian Canal to Inverness, and returning by Aberdeen and Edinburgh. In 1870 he and his wife spent a few days in Harrogate. 1889 was a bumper year — in May the family travelled by the Midland Railway to London for a ten-day holiday, and in early September (perhaps for the cricket festival) they stayed for nine days at the Prince of Wales Hotel in Scarborough.

In 1883 when Francis was sixty-six, he began to plan and build a new house, Haverdale House, near the Swale a mile or so from Crackpot. A large, plain, four-square house, the first quoin was laid in June and they moved in the following year in October. It is remembered that some of the beams from the old Isles Bridge were re-used for it. A walled garden and an orchard were planted with plums (Orleans, Greengage, Magnum Bonum, Victoria, Imperatrice), with apples (Cockpit, Northern Spy, Worcester Pearman, Golden Pippin, Stirling Castle, Keswick Codling), with a Jargonelle pear tree, a May Duke cherry, a walnut tree, gooseberries, and black, white and red currants.

The move made little difference to the family's daily round. Although administering rather than farming, Francis was still overseeing farm work, going to harvest thanksgivings, selling stock at fairs, visiting Hawes frequently, at a church conference in Leeds, at York Castle as a special juror, at a school treat at Rowleth Bottom, presiding at a Conservative meeting at Reeth, at Reeth School Arts Examination, at the public opening of the Melbecks and Grinton Conservative Club Reunion, and at Fair Trade Leagues at Low Row and Haverdale Mill. He became chairman of Reeth District Council, a justice of the peace, and a county councillor for the North Riding.

In 1893 he recorded 'Preparing pedigree of Cattle for Herd Book', but in September eleven years later when he was eighty-seven he sold his herd of Shorthorns. A well-known auctioneer, John Thompson, came from London to preside. Fifty-nine animals made £1,217, an average of £20 12s 8d, only a modest figure. Some were sent to the buyers from Askrigg station and others from Richmond. The entries in the last day book gradually diminish as he approaches his ninetieth year. He died on the 22nd December 1911. His wife had died the year before.

At that time the two daughters were in their thirties and they began a new life. They had been educated by governesses, and the eldest was musical and the younger sister artistic. So they let the farm and house, and went for months on end to live first in rooms in Leeds where they took singing, piano and clarinet lessons at the Leeds College of Music, and attended the Leeds Musical Festival and performances at the Grand Theatre. (Who then from mid-Swaledale was hearing as they were *The Rhinegold* and *The Valkyrie*?) Early in 1914 they embarked on a grand tour of France and Italy lasting from February until May. Frances, who was talented, sketched the Grand Canal at Venice and other scenes. Finally they took a flat in London which allowed time for her to study at the Slade School. But they always returned to Swaledale, eventually to live in a half of Haverdale House. Theirs is a very different story.

Throughout the journals the comments are perhaps disappointingly few. No doubt the diarists' full lives left little time for long entries. After reading them, what lingers in the mind is the work on the farm proceeding in all weathers, the picture of them busy in buildings, house, garden and fields, in Burblet, Middle Ing, Gill Side, Butts Intake, Sunside, harvesting hay and corn with simple tools, tending the stock, devoted to their family, land and dale, and respected and relied on for help by their friends and neighbours. When Frances Garth died at Haverdale House in 1970 aged ninety-two, the Garth family in Swaledale came to an end.

1   Based on the Garth diaries, 1795—1911, lent to us in 1967 by Miss M F Garth and again by
    Mr J L Barker who now holds them; also on recollections of Miss Garth and Mr and Mrs J.
    R. Brown of Low Row.

2   North Yorkshire Registry of Deeds, Vol DK No 77, pp 100-112. The commissioner was
    Alexander Calvert of Richmond.

3   Bloody Wall struck off at right angles to Bloody Vale, a small valley branching west of
    Summer Lodge/ Haverdale Beck. It is so called because of the folk memory of a battle
    fought there. Bones were found when Melbecks Vicarage at the foot of Crackpot Gill was
    built.

4   Plan of the Manor of Healaugh by R Richardson (1770).

5   Plan of the estate of Mr Barnard Garth, son of James Garth, and Richard Garth at Bank
    Heads near Crackpot (1823), lent by Mr J R Brown.

6   *Coates's Herd Book containing the Pedigrees of improved Short-Horned Cattle* was begun in
    1822, and by the 1870s some 900 breeders from all over the country were listed. As Dairy
    Shorthorns they became the indigenous cattle of the Dales until ousted by the Friesians in
    the 1940s and 1950s. The herd books have been lent to us by Mr J A Willis, grandson of
    Thomas Willis, the well-known breeder of shorthorns at Carperby in Wensleydale. The
    Garths' herd books, bound in white vellum, have been sold.

The Lead and Shipping Agent

There were many agents in the mining fields, but the lead and shipping agent was in a different category. Matthew Wadeson was one of a series who over the years officiated at the port of Stockton-on-Tees in the sale and despatch of lead brought from the mines in Swaledale, Arkengarthdale, and sometimes from those in Teesdale and Wensleydale. He kept records of his correspondence, of which two letter-books dated the 5th January 1792 to the 8th September 1808 form the basis of this account.[1]

In the late eighteenth and early nineteenth century there were two other agents in Stockton, the Raisbecks and the crown agent, George Hutchinson, with whom Matthew was on good if distant terms. In February 1792 he wrote of Stockton: 'This is one of the Principal Markets for Lead & the London Merchts have so much from us ... '

Wadeson himself had been connected with the lead trade since the 1770s, and he was well respected both for his integrity and for his knowledge of the mines. When the correspondence begins he was agent for the Pomfret/Denys family, proprietors of the AD mines in Swaledale. He frequently wrote to, and when he was at Fremington near Reeth sometimes met, Peter Denys, then a lead merchant in London who in 1787 had married Charlotte, daughter of Lord Pomfret. In 1794 he was appointed steward to Sir Charles Turner of Kirkleatham near Redcar, part owner by marriage to a Bathurst of the CB mines in Arkengarthdale. Matthew occasionally wrote fulsomely to correspondents, including Lord Darlington of Raby Castle. His lordship's mines in Teesdale at one stage came third in importance to the great AD and CB mines, the source of most of the lead shipped from Stockton, so that these two figure prominently in the correspondence.[2]

Wadeson also had other interests. He was a partner in the Fell End mines in Arkengarthdale and attended pay days. He had shares in some of the ships, and wrote of taking on a shot and gunpowder agency: 'The Season for the Consumption of Shot is coming ... It is a country where much is used for the Moorgame shooting.' And writing of gunpowder, he stated that 'what is used at the Mines ... is considerable as to quantity'. The agency was for the products of Walker Fishwick and Company of Newcastle, of whom he wrote that it was 'One of the completest

Manufacturys in England for the productions from lead viz sheets [rolled lead], shot, Colours for paints etc.'[3]

Matthew's prime concerns were the market price of lead and the safe despatch of it in sailing ships mostly to London, but also to Hull, Newcastle, to Dutch and German ports, and occasionally via the Baltic to Memel in Lithuania and to St Petersburg where new buildings were still going up. Often Hull, a rival market, 'swallows all the production'. His business required daily attention, and troubles arose when he was away from work, sometimes with influenza and once with a broken rib. He kept up a perpetual correspondence with mine owners and lessees, in the early years with Peter Denys in his dual role as proprietor and lead merchant, later with Easterby Hall and Company who leased the CB mines in 1800, with the Stapletons of Richmond, Miles and his son, Thomas, lessees of Hurst mines, Ralph Parke of Low Row in Swaledale (see the chapter *Base Metal*), Sampson George of Middleton Tyas, Lord Darlington's agent and many smaller adventurers.

He wrote frequently and despatched lead often weekly to Walkers Maltby and Company of Red Bull Wharf, London, lead merchants and the chief buyers.[4] In the year 1800 he shipped to that company 14,470 pieces of lead from nine mines using thirteen ships, some making one, some four or five voyages. He also dealt with other London merchants, John Hague, John Ellill, and John Locke and Company, and from time to time with agents in foreign ports. He journeyed to London, Hamburg and Rotterdam, but gives no details. Matthew's was a vital link in the mining industry, for the prosperity of the mines and the then industrial dales dependent on the sale and price of lead.

Stockton then ranked as the chief port between Hull and Newcastle.[5] It lay ten miles from the sea on the north bank of the Tees, whose course was tortuous and the navigable channel narrow. Nonetheless, in 1795 forty-seven vessels were registered there. Brigs, sloops, brigantines, the regular traders and foreign vessels, albeit dependent on the tides, plied up and down it with their multifarious cargoes.[6] When there were difficulties, barges carried goods down the river to where ships were held up. Matthew, a committee man, attended meetings which in 1810 saw navigation improved by a cut from Portrack to Stockton.[7] Ship-builders, a shipping company, sail-cloth manufacturers and roperies flourished. The wharves swarmed with porters, boatmen and ships' crews. In 1794, Peter Denys was building a wharf and putting up new buildings designed by the Richmond architect John Foss (1745-1827). Wadeson wrote to him arranging the pulling down of granaries and letting the brickwork, flooring and roofing, but advises to 'Take the Stone work in Hand ourselves … Our wharf upon Mr Foss's Plan will on considering it come to a very serious Sum. I was in Hopes of accomplishing our first Design for £300 and double the sum I fear will fall far short of Foss's design.'

At that date Middlesbrough, iron masters and the Stockton and Darlington Railway had not yet blossomed (although Matthew lived to see the latter). Sea bathing

The wharves and shipping on the River Tees at Stockton in 1825. Some of the ships would be larger than those berthed here in Matthew Wadeson's day, as the river had been improved by the cut from Portrack to Stockton. Note the racecourse and race meeting in progress on the south bank.

was fashionable with the gentry, and Cargo Fleet, now the name of an iron and steel works, was 'a Creek down our River'. In 1794 Matthew sent a cured Tees salmon to Walkers Maltby and wrote: 'They are accounted very nice either Braised or Boiled. I hope yours will be found so, it was a Choice Fish.' Stockton ceased to be a port in 1859 and eventually lost its custom house so often mentioned in the letters to Middlesbrough.[8]

Merchants expected immediate delivery of lead, so that one of Wadeson's many anxieties was the effect of wintry weather — snow on roads and wharves, and ice on the river. In 1795 the winter was 'more severe than any I remember ... It is again come Easterly & looks stormy as ever the *Joseph & William* is laying in the mouth of our river & the *Hannah* [later damaged by ice] cannot yet proceed.' In the 1801-2 winter, 'The Frost having for a week here lock'd up our River' is a typical report. No wonder that he wrote to Thomas Stapleton on 9 December 1805 'that the sooner [lead] is got down the better'.

Ships were hampered by neap tides, and time and time again windbound by easterlies. On the 1st June 1805 he wrote: 'The weather has been for some time so boisterous & bad, no vessels dared to Venture out, indeed we have in the low part of our River, many Colliers who have come in for shelter ... Vessels are coming round from Whitby to seek loading here.' Ships were blown on shore and many narrowly escaped shipwreck. It was often with some relief that he was able to report that vessels had got to sea: 'Captain Greare sail'd from hence Monday last in the morning & from the prospect I consider he is likely to be with you before long.' Dependent on the westerlies the voyage to Newcastle took one or two days, that to Rotterdam or Emden eight days. Once a ship 'performed wonders being but 36 hours between the River Tees and the Thames'. But at times they sought shelter in Yarmouth Roads and Harwich.

Throughout the period covered by the correspondence, war with France caused hazards at sea, and affected trade and the price of lead. At times, continental ports were closed to English ships and 'neutral bottoms', chiefly Dutch, carried lead and other goods. In 1803 fifteen neutral ships carried 13,238 pieces of lead to Emden. In March 1793, Wadeson was writing to a foundry for ships' guns — four two-pounders and '4 three-pounders & 4 Swevils for Vessels between 90 and 100 tons'. Ships sailed in convoys. In March 1793 'the *Hannah* went to sea ... and joined a large Fleet of Colliers'. In November 1794 he wrote to Peter Denys: 'We are very anxious about the ship [on a voyage to St Petersburg] on Account of French Cruisers on the Coast of Norway.' In January 1804 'a number of our Vessels are carrying Corn & Flour to the different military Stations along the Coast', and later in November 'A privateer has done much mischief on our Coast ... serious fears are entertained for Captain Hansell.' One captain did disappear, captured by the French.

In 1796, Matthew was elected to the first committee to form a volunteer corps which was eventually called the Loyal Stockton Volunteers, and two years later he was writing to Walkers Maltby: 'I know not how the Londoners feel at the threats of the French, but here we are all learning the use of Arms. My House, shop, office and Barges produce 5 Men and my Neighbours all exhibit great Spirit.'

All these troubles are reflected in the day-to-day correspondence. In the early years, whilst mainly engaged in the lead trade, he also dealt in shipments, mostly from Holland, of matts of flax for the sailcloth manufactory, hessian yarn for linen manufacturers in the Stokesley area, cow hides, calf skins and bark for tanning, wine and beer in bottles packed in hampers, flooring laths, rush matting, tarras (mortar), blue millstones, and on two occasions huge gravestones. He ventured a shipment of ten or twelve horses to Hamburg. 'I mean to export a little Hay along with them, so that the diet of Hambro' may be introduced by mixing.' Bales of stockings knitted in the Dales and exported by the Richmond hosiers are briefly mentioned. In 1795 he wrote to Peter Denys that he has obtained 'a Bell of good Tone which I got very reasonable from a Capt trading to Sweden', and in the same year he ordered from Hamburg 'a Kegg or two of the freshest Black Beere ... 'tis for a Minister of his own Parish to apply to Charitable purposes'. But this mixed trade as far as Matthew was concerned faded out by 1803.

Lead was constantly coming down from the mines, a distance of forty or fifty miles or more. At that time it was brought from the smelt mills, in pieces or pigs of lead weighing just over a hundredweight each, on packhorses as far as Richmond and thence following two routes by cart to Stockton, where it was piled up on the wharves ready for shipping. Most was best lead, a little was slag; and Teesdale lead was said to be harder than Swaledale. The pieces were stamped at the mill with marks or marking hammers with the initials of the mine or a cipher for it,[9] and with letters of the alphabet to aid counting by denoting the number, usually 100 or multiples of a hundred for each letter.[10] Four hundred pieces made a 'mark', weighing 24 to 28 tons, and fractions or multiples of this were shipped if possible. Sometimes a ship was kept waiting for pieces to come down to complete a mark.

Known rules of the trade were observed. Lead was sold by the fother, here the Stockton fother of 22 cwt, differing slightly from those of other markets. Although the pieces had been weighed at the mills, they were weighed again on the wharves at a small charge to the buyer, who often sent a representative to attend. When a slight dispute arose, Matthew stated that he used 'a truly poiz'd Beam' and later informed

Weighing pigs of lead at Richmond Station circa 1870, a scene not unlike that taking place on the wharf at Stockton in the early nineteenth century.

an agent that the scales were regularly inspected. On the 7th March 1807 he wrote: 'I hope we shall have no complaint of our weighing Ice for lead.'

Freight charges ranged from 10s to 15s a ton depending on whether lead was taken as ballast or whether it wholly filled a ship at a busy time. There were other various dues: boatage, bills of lading, custom-house duty, sometimes the expense of piling up the pieces, and the agents' commission — 5s a score of pieces for shipping and no bills given, and one per cent for lead bought and bills given. Insurance was the buyer's business, and lead was paid for on receipt by three-monthly or six-monthly bills. Occasionally a piece was lost or wrongly shipped, and had to be sought and brought back. Sometimes if Matthew had bought lead from an old church, as he did, and had it run off into pieces, it was marked at Stockton. In September 1803 a firm 'has had made a Marking Hammer which shall be applied to each pig or bar of lead as we ship it', and in 1804 he remarked that 'They charge very high for special Hammers'. Once three thieves attacked the wharf. Once pigs were stolen in London, and in October 1793 lead was being filched *en route* from the mines. Matthew advised Peter Denys that a handbill offering a reward of twelve, fifteen or twenty guineas for apprehending the thief be printed and posted all along the road.

Carriage, dependent on the jaggers and carriers, presented intractable problems. In December 1795 he reported that 'I find not much lead has come down perhaps the Jaggers are busy in the [mining] field'; and again in July, as the carriers were mostly farmers they were often attending to the harvest. In November 1800, 'On acct of the dearness of Corn & the consequent bad condition & falling off of Horses: we find Lead coming very slow indeed.' Oats were in fact shortly sent to Arken–garthdale.

It was usual to enter into contracts for transport. For instance, on the 10th June 1802, Peter Denys agreed with George and Tobias Cradock of Preston in Wensleydale that they should carry the lead from Old Gang and other mines from Richmond to Stockton at the rate of thirteen guineas for every 400 pigs delivered until March 1803. Denys had struck a good bargain. In the spring of 1801 Matthew had written that the carriage was £14 and that the men were asking £20 or even £25. 'The carriers are all our Masters', he commented.

Seasonal obstacles also plagued him and he wrote similarly: 'We cannot manage the Masters [ships' captains]'. 'None of the regular vessels will take Lead if anything else can be had.' Corn, pork and cheese were the rival cargoes. In September 'from the first offering of Grain we are put on our turns in Shipg Lead & now the Pork Season is also coming … apprehend great difficulty'; and by January, 'The Pork Trade will begin to go off from Stockton to London & Lead begin to play again.' By May 'The season for Pork & Ham is over.' (Pork was packed in salt in casks.) Cheese brought from all the dairying districts to Yarm Fair in late October was shipped a day or two afterwards to London. 'Our Regular Traders are waiting for Yarm Fair to catch the Cheeses. '

Nonetheless, letters concerned with the despatch of lead fill the ledgers and in the second they are freely interspersed with bills of lading. A typical heading for one of these runs for August 1795, 'Character Marks and Weight of 2,650 Ps of Lead Ship'd for P. Denys Esqr to Mr Jas Hague London by Matt Wadeson'. Then follows a list of 500 pieces of AD lead shipped in the *Neptune* — Henry Terry, master; 500 in the *Union* — Chris Barnicle, master; and 1,650 in the *Satisfaction* — Robert Norman, master; a total weight of 2,316 cwt. Wadeson had a share in the brig *Satisfaction,* and the *Neptune* was an old vessel whose captain in 1806 was transferred to a new ship — the *Active.* In October 1797 Captain Greare, master of the *Stockton Packet,* leaving for Hamburg, had obtained and sailed under a Prussian flag. He appears to have landed in trouble for this.

Ships of different burden took different amounts — 1,000 to 3,000 pieces. One Dutch vessel, the *Engelina,* bound for Emden, was so extraordinarily long and narrow that Matthew only committed a shipment of 1,150 pieces to her because it was summer time. One ship was laid on the sands at Portrack (on the Tees) for inspection and repair, and a shipwright was consulted about the *Mary Joseph's* capability of carrying lead, as she was an old vessel not favourable in appearance but with a careful master. 'Coal', Matthew wrote, 'is such a price in Rotterdam that Captain Barrett will only take 200 pieces as ballast (he had rather 150) & the Stocking Bales.' In 1806 a new shipping company formed at Stockton brought competition for ships between the port and London. On the 1st November 1806, Wadeson wrote to Walkers Maltby: 'An opposition is forming to the old Traders ... a general meeting is called for Tuesday ... you shall know what the new Shipping Co have to offer.' 'Now that we have two sets of vessels', he added. But he reiterated that 'Our instructions are to Ship by the first Vessel that sails & that I must do if she is seaworthy.'

The market price of lead, influenced by the London merchants, was naturally of paramount importance. Wadeson needed to know what other agents were offering and learnt prices from people from the Dales, at the coffee house or from other sources. In 1792 it was £20 a fother — 'the first sale of best Lead this season — bought by irregular customers to send to Bremen'. Depressed by the French war, the price in April 1793 fell to £18 10s, and he wrote in that year, 'There are mines which cannot be worked unless lead be at £18 p Fother.' By October 'There is all at once a monstrous bustle to learn how much each holder of Lead has on hand & to know what each will take.' But the price dropped to £17, and in the following spring to £15 and £16.

Following rumours of peace in 1795, the price temporarily rose to £21 but fell again. In January 1797 Matthew wrote, 'I find a resolution among most of the Owners to strike off the hands from the most unprofitable part of their workings. As was the case before Lead fell so much, which I am afraid will effect the poor Miners than the Market.' Five years later, on the 2nd April 1803, Matthew wrote: 'The Hope of seeing £40 & of living for 10 years to come (for I take good care of myself)

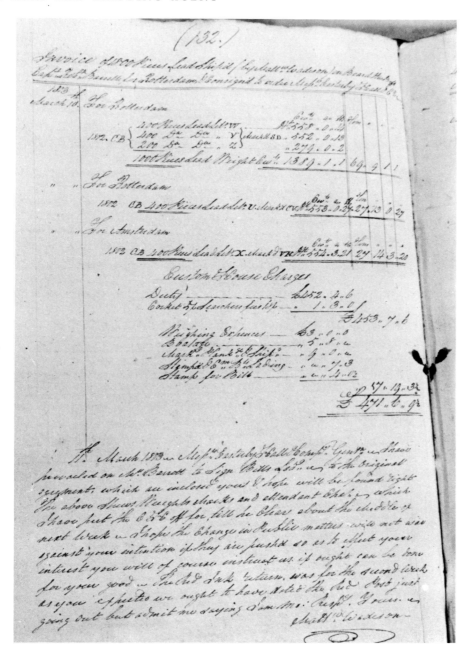

A page from Matthew Wadeson's ledger, March 1803: a bill of lading for 1,800 pieces of CB lead shipped by Matthew Wadeson on board the Bess, *captained by Robert Barrett, bound for Rotterdam and Amsterdam.*

but fear I shall not be so happy as to see Lead in that interval worth £60.' He never did. In March 1805 he was 'stagger'd at the price' (£32), and a day or two later wrote 'the price of Lead is reported as rapidly advancing where it has to end I know not but fear like all extremes 'twill not last'. However, the price rose to £40 and stayed there until early in 1806 it slowly began to decline.

The inflated price, never reached again, had the effect as Matthew said of 'making all Men Miners wherever the Metal can be won to pay & wide will be the field'. Many new names appear in the second book, but at the same time mine owners and lessees increased the common practice of buying up small parcels of ore from mining adventurers to smelt and sell at a profit, thus undermining Matthew's agency. Nonetheless he wrote: 'I wish Mine adventurers always to receive the utmost that can be obtained from his hazardous & sometimes hard earned product.'

In December 1799 Wadeson wrote: 'Hall & Co of Newcastle have at last got agreed for a Lease of the CB Mines consequently we may expect great change.' This was true in many directions. The firm was Easterby Hall and Company, who as the new lessees in Arkengarthdale pursued a vigorous policy. There were two Hall brothers, Walter, whom Wadeson found 'gentlemanly and pleasant', and Frederick, the dominant partner and one of the foremost figures in the mining history of the dales, of whom he commented, 'I have met with some reverse traits'.[11]

In 1803 the company had passed through a crisis following the failure of the Surtees, Burdon and Brandling Bank of Newcastle. In August they began to pay wages weekly instead as was customary half-yearly in order to attract more miners, and,when lead began to rise in price, Frederick adopted new tactics to keep up the momentum. He bought up lead and sold it direct to London merchants, thus avoiding commission. 'This is certainly mischievous to the Trade as it makes it difficult to come at the real value of Lead at our Market', Matthew wrote, and again in August 1806, 'the tricks play'd off by Easterby Hall & Co of late, were such as puzl'd both buyers & sellers'. The arrival of this enterprising firm had another impact. They brought in a 'vast influx of strangers from the mining districts of the western parts of Northumberland, and the neighbouring borders of Durham, Westmoreland and Cumberland', and as a result the Swaledale dialect was affected and lost 'many expressions and comprehensive words'.[12]

One of Wadeson's recognised duties was to report at least fortnightly on the state of the mines to the merchants. As an agent both for the AD and the CB mines for a few years before 1800, he had an opportunity to visit them twice yearly at midsummer and in November for pay days. This took him away to the Dales for about a week. At these times, sales of lead escalated in order to have funds in hand. In June 1795 he wrote of the CB mines, 'We have had a very heavy pay indeed — our quota £1,957 1s. 4d.', and the following July it was £1,890 15s 6d.

The produce of the mines constantly fluctuated, and tallies with the known history of new levels being driven or new smelting mills being built. In March 1792

Matthew wrote, 'Our stock for the Spring sales was small the whole not exceeding 8000 Ps. I have known it 4 times that Qty.' A letter in June states that 'the AD Mines are now very good the CB rather better than they have been & the rest in that quarter produce as usual especially Hurst'.

In April 1794 he admonished Mr Blake Delaval of Hamburg, 'the produce of their Mines [the AD] being above 20,000 Ps annually think of that & avail yourself of it'. And in July, 'The AD comes down now at the rate of 1000 Ps weekly.' In August 1802 'There is in the produce of the AD Mines a very great falling off', but by September he was expecting AD lead to be very great in quantity, and in October 'Mr Denys is forwarding down AD Lead very fast & will for 3 or 4 Weeks to come after which time 2 or 3 Ps a week is all that can be expected. Now it comes at the rate of 6 or 700 Ps a week. 'Tis done to clear out their Mills of an unprecedented accumulation while the Mines were rich.' In August 1805, 'The Surrender Mine (of which Mr Denys has his part with Messrs Chaytor & Breare as lessees & the Earl &

The ruins of Old Gang smelting mill, Swaledale (mid-1930s).

others their part as lessors) is very rich at present.' Surrender adjoined the Old Gang.

In January 1799 he wrote, 'I am sorry to say at present there is great reason to fear that the CB mines are done — the prospect for the Proprietors is a gloomy one.' But on the 10th September 1803 following the change to lessees, Easterby Hall, he wrote to Walkers Maltby that 'I was in the Field [CB Mines] and witnessed such heaps of Ore being brought from the undersets, or lower Beds — as none in the way of mining expected … they have from one level brought Ore that would Yield a Mark of Lead in 48 or 50 Hours, that must have been a Day & Night by Chance, when way gates were cleared out — I think … the great New Mill is getting to work, I expect to see Lead come down very fast.'

Later he says that the new mill with six hearths will be ready by the middle of March 1804. This was the CB smelt mill built by Easterby Hall by the side of the road in Arkengarthdale, the ruins of which can still be seen. In October, 'Much Lead has been sent from Arkendale Mills lately … 6 marks to this place & one to Hull.' Later in December 1806 he wrote, 'I have just been inform'd by one from the Dales E. H. & Co have within Ten days from this, Cut in Danby Levil something very Rich in ore & what is likely to yield beyond ought they have cut before.' In May 1807 he reported that 'They made arrangements of their Smelters to go on at a Mark a Week, but of late they have not been able to make half the Qty.'

Matthew harboured no illusions about Dales weather. From time to time he explained that slow deliveries of lead were caused by frost and snow which hindered washing and smelting. In a dry time too (seldom mentioned), lack of water brought to a standstill the water wheels which motivated the bellows fanning the fires on the hearths of the mills. Once he speaks of 'my Arkendale Habilaments … I have been reduced to a Flannel Collar.' In October 1806 he purposed 'going to the Mines in the Dales beyond Richmond', but gave up because 'The Weather of late has been so rainy I cannot get up for I am a Rheumatic Subject so cannot bear well to be wet to the Skin.' This sadly compares with a November morning two years earlier when 'I Left my Bed this morning after receiving it [a letter from Walkers Maltby] at ½ past 2 o'clock & rode near 60 miles to no purpose finding Mr B had gone to Harrogate.'

Following on new leases, new exploitation, but chiefly inflated prices and effects of war, change overtook Matthew's business. In 1801 Peter Denys had by indenture assigned his interests as a lead merchant to John Locke and Company for twenty-one years. Denys agreed both to send them lead from Old Gang and to persuade his customers to trade with the new company, which paid 12s 6d over and above the market price per fother for the privileges.[13] As a result Matthew regularly shipped AD lead to Lockes, but the agreement did not last the full term. It meant, however, that Matthew's contact with Peter Denys diminished, and in December 1807 he wrote to Walkers Maltby that 'Mr Denys keeps all to himself'.

Easterby Hall dropped him altogether. In October 1804 he wrote: 'My employers

Easterby Hall are taking their Lead to another wharf'. 'All these innovations are I fear hurtful to both sides of the trade. I mean sellers as well as buyers at least what I have well observ'd in near 30 Years experience of Lead concerns give me to think so.' However, in October 1805 Matthew was offering his services and monthly reports on the mines to a new London lead merchant, John Ellill. The association did not last, for Ellill transferred his custom to Leonard Raisbeck, and on the 4th April 1807 Matthew wrote to him that 'I am without any of your regarded favours'. But he was still writing frequently to Walkers Maltby, reporting on custom house clearances and shipping lead.

Ralph Parke was one who mostly dealt with him throughout, but in May 1808 he was about to part with his interest in mines to Thomas Hopper, a Newcastle lead merchant. Thomas Stapleton also kept up his association, and on the 28th October 1807 Matthew wrote to him: 'If I had known of your wants in the way of Candles, would have recommended a maker in London would have used you well.' By now, too, he was dealing with Henry Calvert of Redmire in Wensleydale, agent for Lord Bolton's estate and its mines — Bobscar and others. 'I am wishful', he wrote somewhat piously, 'to receive & take Charge of every man's Lead that can be prevail'd on to send it me down — but never to buy his Lead when any other buyer can offer him a better price for it.'

Owing to Napoleon's blockade of Continental and Russian ports and the start of the Peninsular war, throughout 1807 the value of lead fell rapidly until in April 1808 it was £23. That month Matthew wrote to Walkers Maltby that 'We have no dealings at the Mines, they are turning off all hands, that are winning Ore above a certain rate pr Fodr for many workings that of late have yielded very well, since Lead got below £30, are sinking money very fast indeed … A very considerable part of what comes to this Market [apart from the big mines] is from the undertakings of Mining Adventurers whose narrow means are not equal to the difficulties which times like these bring on them.'

However, when the letters end on the 8th September 1808, trade was brisk again, and the price had risen to £34 or £35 a fother. 'If the Spaniards are favour'd by any Change in Austria & Russia much may be hoped for.'

Matthew, although well aware of the importance of price, could hardly foresee that even as near as the slump of the 1830s and certainly in the 1880s the fall to sometimes £11 or £12 a fother and other factors would bring about the end of the industry, throw hundreds of people out of work in many dales, and cause migration of families from their homelands on a heartbreaking scale.

1   Based on two letter books, 5th January 1792 to 25th October 1800, and 24th October 1800 to 8th September 1808, written by Matthew Wadeson of Stockton-on-Tees, lead and shipping agent, now lodged at the North Yorkshire County Record Office.

2   The AD group of mines on the north side of Swaledale included Old Gang, Lownathwaite,

Blakethwaite, Swinnergill, Keldside, etc, and were named after Alexander Denton, a Wharton trustee. The CB mines in Arkengarthdale were named after Charles Bathurst, grandson of Dr John Bathurst and High Sheriff of Yorkshire in 1727.

3   Walkers Fishwick and Co of Newcastle-upon-Tyne were started in 1778 as manufacturers of white lead by the Walkers, ironmasters of Rotherham. Walkers Fishwick built the famous shot tower at Elswick, Newcastle, in 1797, and later changed their partnership to Walkers Ward and Parker, with whom Wadeson continued to deal. Information kindly supplied by Mr D Rowe and Dr W A L Seaman.

4   Walkers Maltby and Co of London were part of the same partnership, and Thomas Maltby was in charge of the wharf on the Thames built in 1785-6. When the price of lead fell, Maltby was blamed.

5   See M le Guillou, *A History of the River Tees* (1978) pp 1-8.

6   J Brewster, *The Parochial History and Antiquities of Stockton-on-Tees* (1829), p 201. Quoting custom house returns, Brewster gives 2,818 tons 10 cwt of lead sent coastwise to London from Stockton, and 522 tons 8 cwt exported in 1794.

7   T Richmond, *Local Records of Stockton and Neighbourhood* (1868).

8   T Sowler, *A history of the town and borough of Stockton-on-Tees* (1972), p 302.

9   In July 1771, 'Robert Buckle blacksmith made a new mark for Lead ... which went to Swinnergill Mill'. Parke diary in the authors' possession. This mark was used by Wadeson for all the bills of lading for Parke's lead. The character mark for the AD mines was a monogram.

10   A set of marks or marking hammers with the letters of the alphabet on them was kept at the smelt mill. At Whitaside mines they were small marks or stamps hit with a hammer to mark the pigs of lead kept in slots in a special box. Or they were hammers with the initials on the head used in the mines in lower Wensleydale to be seen at the Dales Countryside Museum at Hawes.

11   In a pamphlet *An Appeal to the Poor Miner* written and published by Frederick Hall (second edition 1818), Thomas Maltby is blamed for keeping down the price of lead and in consequence the wages paid to the miners.

12   Captain John Harland, *A Glossary of Words used in Swaledale, Yorkshire,* published by the English Dialect Society in 1873 when Harland was over eighty.

13   Copy of indenture, Lord Pomfret and Peter Denys to J Locke and Co, now lodged at the North Yorkshire County Record Office.

A Country Printer

In 1976 a printing works in the market town of Hawes at the head of Wensleydale changed hands, and a collection of type, hand presses, old posters and much besides, accumulated over 138 years, was disposed of. During that time, five printers had officiated in all. One, W Hiscock, from 1887 to 1917 published a *Wensleydale and Swaledale Almanack,* now valuable. A modern printer, using the latest machines, has followed on.

The press, with a shop attached for the sale of books and stationery goods, was started in 1838 by Fletcher Clarke, then aged twenty. He was the son of the Hawes postmaster, Christopher Clarke, who was also the proprietor of the White Hart Hotel in the town. Three years later, on the 1st January 1841, he embarked on what was to become an ambitious venture. He published 1,000 free copies of *Clarkes's Original Monthly Advertiser* for the market towns of Hawes, Leyburn, Middleham, Askrigg, Sedbergh, Kirkby Stephen, and also for Dent and Garsdale. Situated as it was near the heads of several dales, Hawes served a wide area (as it still does), and copies of the sheet were delivered to the above places to agents who undertook distribution.

The success of the first printing was such that on the 30th January 1,500 free copies with a slightly different title, *Clarke's Monthly Advertising Journal,* were circulated. On the first page of the double sheet is an announcement to the effect that stamped copies were to be published at first at a price of 2½d if called for at the office and 5s 6d annually if sent by post. Eventually, although free copies were still circulated, it was possible to buy the sheet at 2d a copy or 3s a year. So, there developed the *Wensleydale Advertiser,* the first stamped and, therefore, the first legal newspaper in the North Riding, published fortnightly for five years from January 1844 to the beginning of January 1849.[1]

The paper which Fletcher Clarke edited was printed at his office in the Holme, Hawes. (He had started the business in the marketplace and he himself lived at Gayle.) It was a double sheet, foolscap folio, 8¾ inches by 13½ inches, increasing in size in later years to 10 inches by 16 inches. He adopted the format of already established journals by printing advertisements, often of sales, on the front page, followed on other pages by an editorial, local intelligence under the headings of

Hawes in the 1840s. An elegant lithograph by C J Greenwood was published by the Wensleydale
Advertiser. *This is taken from it.*

places, articles on general topics, a gardener's calendar, a report on the weather,
and poetry usually on the back page. Births, marriages, deaths and market news
appeared in every copy, and as the years passed more and more space was occupied
by anonymous, sometimes scurrilous, letters.

In one of his editorials Fletcher Clarke expressed the wish 'to write about our
own loved dales as much as may be possible', but local pride did not deter him from
criticising the state of the town and occasionally the habits of the people. In his first
editorial he writes of 'The simple unsophisticated manners and customs of the dwellers in the country ... their attachment to their localities — the continuance of ancient usages, and unwillingness to admit innovation — peculiarly distinguish them
as a class ... Here may be found that primitive order of society which is fast giving
way to the giant sweep of modern enlightenment.'

His expressed views were by and large high-minded and progressive. He deplores
snobbery, but writes of the 'peasantry' and the 'tenantry', and besides is painfully
coy about 'the fair sex'. We suspect that he was often dismayed by petty gossip and
viewpoints. He writes ' ... a mouth which speaks ill of its neighbours is an engine of

The White Hart Hotel, Hawes, circa 1870. The sign over the door reads: 'G. and J. Blades. Licensed to retail wines French & British spirits Ale Porter & Tobacco. Licensed Post House.'

strife in the care of a fool'. He must also have courted unpopularity by rejecting letters and poems sent in for publication. He says, 'A great number of poetical effusions are again received. Some of them quite below par.' Once stones were thrown at his windows in Gayle.

In the 1840s Hawes was a thriving growing market town with a population of about 1,600. In Elizabethan times it had been divided into East and West Hawes, each occupied by the clans of Routh and Metcalfe, nine families in each.[2] In the mid-seventeenth century Gayle was a larger place than Hawes. But having been granted a market charter in 1700, Hawes was successfully replacing Askrigg only five miles down the dale as the market town for upper Wensleydale. The editor commented in February 1844, 'There are few places we imagine, which have risen so rapidly from a state of obscurity to comparative respectability.' The burst of prosperity had followed the re-routing of and the arrival of turnpike roads, in particular the Richmond to Lancaster via Ingleton, the Askrigg to Kendal via Sedbergh, and the Askrigg to Kirkby Stephen, all of which linked Hawes with the outside world.

What do we learn about Hawes and upper Wensleydale from this unique record, a local paper? Not by any means a full picture in terms of local or social history. Many articles are so verbose as to be unreadable. There is no direct mention of leadmining or of handknitting, for which in the latter case Hawes was a centre. It is rather snippets of information which have to be picked out, plus occasional lengthy pieces of value: the history of Yorebridge Grammar School; an account of the origin of Askrigg Hill Fair; proposals for the routes of new railways; and glimpses of the manners of the times. Most of these are not to be found elsewhere.

At that date and in the immediate future the appearance of the town hardly matched up to its progress, but change was imminent. Old ling-thatched cottages had gone but were remembered. The rebuilding of the church was being bruited, but the old church with a bell turret standing close to the main street was not pulled down and a new church built until 1850. Congregational and Methodist chapels were built in the same decade, and a new national school was opened. General conditions reveal too rapid a growth and want of supervision. Lacking a resident member of the police force, petty burglaries occurred, beggars regularly haunted the town, highway robbery was not unknown, the streets were dirty and the shambles in the market place an eyesore.

One difference between then and now was the presence of several local landowners who had lived there for generations. In the 1840s there were the Metcalfes of Ings House and Ashes, the Harrisons of Hawes, the Allens, Rouths and Whaleys of Gayle, the Balderstons, parsons and surgeons of Sedbusk, and the Coultons of Burtersett. G G Coulton, the medieval scholar, was descended from the latter. Concerts, elegant dances and a thriving subscription library flourished.

A host of farmers and craftsmen, including a clockmaker, a cooper, a nailmaker, a saddler and a corn miller, filled the middle ranks, whilst in this firmly-stratified society the poor and unfortunate eked out a living as servants, labourers, knitters, quarrymen and colliers. Subscriptions for the distribution of money, oatmeal, and coal to the poor were usual in winter. The activities of friendly societies — the Oddfellows, the Foresters, the Equitable and Benevolent and others — were from time to time reported.

A first ledger, still extant, was kept by Fletcher Clarke before he started the *Advertiser*.[3] It reveals the names of many of his customers — whilst the majority lived in Hawes, others came with or sent orders from Dent, Sedbergh, Garsdale, Muker, Askrigg, Leyburn, Middleham, Langstrothdale and Kirkby Stephen. Parsons and others buy religious books — Mrs A Metcalfe of Hawes pays 5s for *Hints to a Clergyman's Wife*. Surgeons buy the *Lancet*, tailors the *Gazette of Fashion*. Paul Nixon, sculptor at the marble works at Dent, buys *Turner's Picturesque Tour* for 7s 6d, and books on design for monuments. The Rev W Balderston of Sedbusk and of St Johns College, Cambridge, soon to become master of Yorebridge Grammar School, buys several numbers of *French in Four Months* and *German Self-Taught*. Mrs Alderson of

Askrigg buys amongst many items *The Vicar of Wakefield* costing 2s 9d, and six numbers of *Nicholas Nickleby*, then being published, for 6s. Auctioneers buy advertisements from him. Mr Grose, an itinerant actor, orders playbills, and Mr Kay, dancing master of Askrigg, fifty circulars for 2s 9d.

At the same time, Fletcher Clarke records subscriptions and fines for the library and the librarian's annuity of 5s. He supplies it with books and magazines, such as Lockhart's *Life of Scott* for £4 4s, the fourth volume of Southey's *The Doctor* for 10s 6d, and *Frazer's Magazine*, the *Edinburgh Review*, the *Atheneaum* and *Chamber's Journal*. He runs an account with the music publishers, Simpkins Marshall, adding up to £43 19s 1d, for eight months, and states that he has a book and music parcel arriving monthly from London. He also acts as agent for the *Leeds Intelligencer* and for firms which bind books. He sells scissors, paper in reams, quills, steel pens, wafers, inks, sealing wax, slates, packs of cards, almanacs, card cases, mathematical instruments, prints of Hardraw Scar at 4s and much besides. His office is a depot

'Hardraw Scar', published by Fletcher Clarke, editor of the Wensleydale Advertiser, *at Hawes.*

for the placing of advertisements, and he acts as an intermediary in finding positions for apprentices.

In that era of the railway mania, advertisements of the proposed routes of new railways fill pages of the *Advertiser*. The route of the York and Glasgow Union Railway was to start at Thirsk and pass through Bedale and Hawes to Westmorland to join the Lancashire and Carlisle Railway. Others were being surveyed from Ripon to Skipton via Coverdale, and from Settle to Hawes, to Muker, Reeth and Richmond. In 1845 Middleham was inundated with surveyors, runners and speculators, and at Hawes itself assessors were based to find out the likely amount of traffic. The editor frequently weighed up the pros and cons: the damage to valuable land, the intrusion of rough workmen, the disturbance of the peace; and on the credit side the increase in trade, and in the value of land, more visitors, the establishment of manufacture and the opening of quarries. He writes of 'a money-getting generation … with a remorseless hungering after their prey. The scouts of the advancing army of railway speculators rush about in every direction, up hill and down dale.' But after all the schemes, none materialised, and it took another forty years for the railway to reach Hawes, and then it closed down seventy-six years later in 1954.

The turnpikes had by no means lost their importance. Meetings of the trustees of the Richmond to Lancaster were often advertised, as well as auctions for the letting of the toll bars. It was reported on the 10th October 1848 that Holly Hill Gate, Bellerby Lane End Gate, Ballowfield Bridge Gate, Bainbridge Gate and Hawes Gate were all let for £385 above the expense of collecting the tolls.

Carriers' carts, packhorses (never mentioned but they existed) and the Wensleydale Royal Mail Coach provided general transport. The latter, newly started, was news. It left Northallerton and later Bedale on the arrival of the London mail train each morning and, travelling by Leyburn and West Witton, reached Hawes at 2pm. More than once a horse fell, and on one occasion the coach was benighted in a snowstorm at Mossdale Moor at the head of the dale near the Guide Post Inn (now the Moorcock), so that the coachman had to walk to Hawes with the mail and back again. In the summer months on three days a week 'a new conveyance built expressly for the purpose' went forward from Sedbergh to Kendal. The fare from Northallerton to Kendal was 20s inside and 13s 6d outside. Cushions 'of a very soft description' were recommended for outside. 'Great numbers' of tourists are reported travelling through to the Lake District in August, and lists of names are given.

These passers-by annoyed the editor and prompted him to extol the superior beauties of Wensleydale, 'the rich variety of shade, the deep blue of the heather and the dark green of the mountain fern, with the bright verdant pasturage'. W G J Barker, author of *The Three Days of Wensleydale*, contributes letters, poems and nature notes. One of his verses reads:

> *To southern climes let others roam—*
> *more dear to me my rugged home;*

A page of the Wensleydale Advertiser *for the 8th July 1845, showing advertisements for proposed railways.*

And whilst my will continues free
My dwelling on the hills shall be!

The sentiments may be similar but the quality compares sadly with the poems Emily Brontë was writing at much the same time.

We read of the many oak trees once growing round Bolton Castle, and the holly trees then being cut down in lower Coverdale. Salmon were caught in the river near Aysgarth, and this coveted fish, being plentiful in June 1844, was selling at 7d to 8d a pound. Poaching of trout was rife. The newly-formed Hawes and Abbotside Angling Association was then piling the river, that is driving in piles to prevent the illegal use of nets dragged over the bed. It was a sporting countryside, with hare coursing, otter hunting, grouse and duck shooting. Numbers of swans, duck and wild geese are often reported on Semerwater in January.

It was also an age of enlightenment in agriculture and the start of many agricultural shows. Both Leyburn and the Wensleydale Agricultural Societies promoted exhibitions as they were then called. The latter gave a £1 prize for six new milk cheeses, and both awarded prizes to the labourer who had brought up and placed out to service the greatest number of children without parochial assistance, and the bachelor or spinster who had lived the longest in one place.

Small items link up with national affairs. In January 1844 influenza was raging in Hawes, and in March 1846 smallpox was 'prevalent in the neighbourhood'. In that and the following year, groups of emigrants from Swaledale passed through the town on their way to Liverpool bound for the United States. An agent advertised cheap passages to Australia, the Cape of Good Hope, and a passage to America for £5. In April 1848 the editor frequently refers to foreign news of revolutions and mentions Communism as defined by Louis Blanc, the French politician and historian.

One editorial weighs up the pros and cons of capital punishment and deplores the degrading scenes at public executions. Another regrets the apathy shown towards changes in the postal service 'in these go-ahead days when time is money'. One complaint states that the Mail Ride to Dent, twelve miles away by the old road over Widdale Fell, had been discontinued without warning, so that letters from Hawes to Dent and Sedbergh were having to go round by York, Leeds, Manchester, Lancaster and Kendal — a state of affairs comparable with today.

On the 27th May 1845, the Rev Charles Kingsley was appointed to the stall of St Anthony in the collegiate church of Middleham. Only a month before we read of a sweep carrying his boy across Middleham Bridge in his soot sack to avoid paying the penny toll. Did Kingsley hear of this? On the 31st May 1841 it is reported that a sword was found in Cotterdale during draining operations. This and its well-preserved scabbard, dating from the Iron Age, also raises interesting speculation. (It is now in the British Museum.)

It is recorded in the *Advertiser* that the Loyal Dales Volunteers, a body formed for home defence in the Napoleonic Wars, wore scarlet uniforms, and that they were

A half page of Clarke's Monthly Advertising Journal *for 31st May 1841. Gayle Mill is
advertised to be let or sold, and Mossdale Moor Fair to be held behind the Guide Post Inn.*

summoned by a false alarm, a ling fire on Penhill, where there was a beacon, to
muster at Middleham. In January 1844 the famous West Riding soprano, Mrs Sun-
derland, sang at a concert in Leyburn and was rapturously received. An advertisement of a boarding school at Middleham states that 'each pupil will be provided
with a single bed' and that 'the pupils are treated with parental kindness'. *(Nicholas
Nickleby* was perhaps having its effect.) At Askrigg with a population of 700, 26
people average more than 83 years of age and 26 average 74 years. There are cases of
many applications, often poignant, for the maintenance of illegitimate children.

Corn and woollen mills are working at Hawes and Gayle respectively. A boy loses an
arm in a machine at the latter. Bainbridge corn mill, burnt down in 1830, suffers

another small fire. Old people remember being hired at East Witton hirings, for the village was once a market town with a charter granted to the monks of Jervaulx Abbey in 1307.

Then, a popular annual event started in 1840 was the Leyburn Shawl Tea Festival, which was an occasion applauded by the editor as an advocate of temperance. For this paths were laid out, a marquee erected, triumphal arches adorned the way there and two bands played. In 1845, 1,000 people drank tea in the marquee, and 2,000 people promenaded up and down or later enjoyed country dancing. At night, balls — with quadrilles, waltzes, and the latest dance, the polka, then the rage — continued until after midnight at the Leyburn inns.

A poem on Wensleydale appearing on the 24th September 1844 gives prophetic glimpses of the future. Subtitled 'A Dream' by Zeta, the poet pictures the dale full of trade and commerce, the thoroughfares crowded with people, pickpockets at large, and on Penhill a crowd watching people sick of life on earth going to the moon in a huge balloon.

Fletcher Clarke retired as editor and proprietor in June 1848, 'with the conviction of having — amongst all his errors — intentionally offended no-one, he resigns with complacency yet gratitude an office which is as difficult to fulfil as its rewards are certain'. We are not told the reason for his resignation. In 1851, Fletcher Clarke of Hawes, wine merchant, was bankrupt. He lived in Dyehouse Garth and had two daughters aged six and one. Christopher Clarke had died in 1840.

However, after an interval Thomas Blades took over as editor and printer on the 4th July. He remained printer for four years, but only kept on the paper for four months. *The Wensleydale Advertiser* ceased publication with number 133 on the 2nd January 1849, the same day on which it was first published in 1844. A brave venture ended.

Copies of the paper are rare — a few of the first *Monthly Advertisers*, odd numbers, one volume for 1845, and two sets of bound volumes both with one year missing are preserved in the dale. A complete file except for the last number is in the British Library's Newspaper Library in London.

1   Based on two sets of *The Wensleydale Advertiser*, 1844—49, lent by Mr T C Calvert and the Wensleydale School, Leyburn. Copies of the paper are rare, and the above are incomplete but complement each other. A single volume (1845) is in the authors' possession. A complete file except for the last number is in the British Library's Newspaper Library in London.

2   Corporation of London Records Office, Guildhall, Survey RCE Rentals Box 7-6, and Rentals No 56 Yorkshire Richmond and Middleham 1658. This gives 17 names under Hawes and 51 under Gayle.

3   Accounts kept by Fletcher Clarke from 1838 to 1845. Ledger lent to us by Mason Bros, Hawes.

A Nineteenth-Century Blacksmith

A series of small notebooks, some of the top edges of the leaves brittle and browned by fire, have been roughly sewn together between the worn leather-covered boards of an old book with the date 1849 in gold-tooled lettering on the spine. The date relates to John Calvert, then smith at Gunnerside in Swaledale, several of whose ledgers and day books have been preserved. But in this book day-by-day entries, written in now-faded ink in spidery handwriting, record work done, added to here and there by personal notes as in a diary, for two years 1871 and 1872, in the life of John's son, David Calvert (1819-1906), master blacksmith of Gunnerside.[1]

As we turn the pages we are transported to a Swaledale of rather more than a hundred years ago. It is a hermetic world of folk known by their bynames, of agricultural implements and domestic utensils now obsolete and described by forgotten dialect words spelt phonetically. The life of the inhabitants peeps out in kaleidoscopic fashion, and the smith's customers go about their daily business. Each season brings its own tasks and events. The smith's work, then indispensable to the smooth running of farm and household, was not by any means confined to the shoeing of horses, but meant the repair of anything from clogs to shandreys (carts with springs) or the provision of 'heters' for 'smouthing' irons to kitchen ranges. Also as was the custom for craftsmen and leadminers alike, David owned three acres of land for a cow and a Galloway, so that morning and evening milkings began and ended the day.

In the 1870s the leadmines, recovered from the slump of the 1830s, temporarily flourished with lead at £20 even £23 a fother. Then, apart from a few craftsmen and farmers, a shopkeeper or two, schoolmasters and a policeman, the occupation was leadmining. There were in Gunnerside and on the hills above it 151 houses and 155 leadminers and eight ore-washers. Only twenty of them had land, ranging from one to ten acres. The women, apart from a knitter, two dressmakers and a nurse, found their employment as domestic servants.[2] As we should say now, it was a classic case of lack of diversification in employment, and it was a world in the process of breaking up. Already warning had been given. Many people had left or were leaving for the United States, Durham coal fields or Lancashire cotton towns.

David himself was self-employed except for weekly work, soon to finish,

Gunnerside, showing Gunnerside Gill on the left and miners' cottages on the hillside above. The smithy is on the extreme left above a glimpse of white road.

undertaken for the Whitaside Mining Company and occasional jobs for other companies and partnerships. We may trace the fortunes of his family, for as his descendants say, 'David was fearful for putting things down'. He had married Margaret Woodward and they had nine children, five girls and four boys — Mary, William, John, Elizabeth, David, Margaret, James, Adeline (Addy) and Charlotte, most of them eventually to be scattered far and wide. His cousin, another David Calvert, had until recently been landlord of the King's Head at Gunnerside, as his father had been before him. Other unrelated Calverts were joiners and a second family, John Calvert and his son, James, were also blacksmiths.

In 1871 David was fifty-one. Mary the eldest daughter had left home to take up a post as housekeeper at Hurworth near Darlington. William was married to Peggy Brunskill and had two small children. John aimed to be a school teacher. Elizabeth, then nineteen, was a domestic assistant, David aged sixteen a blacksmith, and the four younger children down to Charlotte aged three were at school.

It is remembered that Peggy Brunskill's mother and father lived at Dirty Spot, an

David Calvert and his son James in the 1890s, shoeing a horse at Gunnerside Smithy.

up and down, one of three cottages in a row, on the hill above Gunnerside where there were then thirty-two scattered dwellings, mostly miners' cottages and one or two farms. Theirs was the simple, kindly nature to be found in people living in remote places. He was a leadminer, handy in the house, for his wife suffered 'a kind of illness'. But she was nonetheless a very proud woman and always wore a fancy cap with ribbons. Everyone loved to visit, 'for no-one baked like mi grandmother'. Brunskill used to take bread and cheese to the mine, and returning home, if he heard of a neighbour's illness, he immediately set out to offer help.

At Gunnerside, traffic going up and down the dale takes a sharp bend over the bridge spanning the beck, missing the smithy which is up a cul-de-sac where water flows out of the arms of the gill above. Steep hillsides, with tracks to former miners' cottages perched in defiance of easy approach, tower above. At the end was then the corn mill run by the Percivals, so that this was a busy corner. The two-storied smithy stands well back from the beck. Its door, a convenient testing place for horn burns for sheep and marks for individuals and mining companies, makes a palimpsest of the dale's history. Inside the two hearths are dimly-lit and on the left is a stand for horses. On the door of an oak corner cupboard is a tattered poster depicting the winners of the Derby and the St Leger in 1848, and on the inside a yellowing hand-bill advertising Reeth New and Old Fairs for the year 1852. All around and hanging on the beams are the accumulated clutter of obsolete and present-day tools of a smithy.

When David began his day book on the 2nd January, he and his third son, an-other David, were each at work on a hearth. Tan Hill coals glowed fiercely in the draught of the bellows as they pumped the handles. In the top corner of the page we read 'On with John's box', that is making hinges and iron bands for a wooden box. John, having started his education at the Wesleyan school in the village (for the family were Wesleyans), was leaving the dale to be a schoolmaster. At Gunnerside there were two schools, the National and the Wesleyan, necessary for the many children, 130 of school age, from the generally large families of those days. (In 1995 there are thirty-three children at Gunnerside school, which serves the upper dale.)

That day, William, a fully-fledged smith, was working at Hurst leadmines, but was planning to leave the dale. David must have thought of the others at home or as yet at school. He and his family faced an uncertain future with stoic composure.

The third entry is headed 'Wedensday Muker Fair Day January 4th'. The fair, known as Muker Aud Roy, was one of two in the year for sheep and cattle, accom-panied by stalls, sports, and old-fashioned dances at night. That day everyone in the upper dale who could was bound for Muker, but David himself was at work all day. We read:

Elizabeth Buxton [The Buxtons were a well-known Wesleyan family]

Girth put on pig tub and 1 old girth Altering [Girths were iron bands put on a wooden tub]	1s 3d
John Metcalfe Spring End Pair Clogs *Carkered* [irons put on soles]	7d
Anty Coty 2 plates put on Clogs	2d
Isebella Renoldson [innkeeper] 4 Shoes Sharping [sharps put on horses' shoes in frost]	1s 0d
Simon Dougill [builder and stonemason] lug [ear] for pail	2d

GOOD

The asides with which David enlivened his accounts could only mean that in this case, despite the attractions of the fair, he had had a good day.

Two days later an entry headed 'Whitaside' records sharpening a jumper (borer) for 'Miners Hunt', and as only one other entry appears for that day David may well have set off for Whitaside. Coursing with trencher-fed hounds, often kept by the miners, and hound trails offered exhilarating sport, running and jumping over steep hillsides and rock-strewn moorland, for men who spent much time underground.

On the 10th January we read 'Edwars Broadrak [Broderick] Brass Screw for line Drawing insterment 6d.' The Brodericks of Spring End and Summer Lodge, across the valley from Gunnerside, were yeomen of long standing, and Edward was a land surveyor. Later David mended Edward a gig shaft assisted by William Alderson, the shoemaker, who put on a leather cover. On other days he provided the same customer with a new *swape* [handle] for a coffee mill, and supplied the iron parts for three coal waggons probably for Tan Hill pit. On the same 10 January he wrote: 'David Sam Isabella Pair New Tongs & Poker 3s. 6d.' Swages for making pokers still hang from the beams of the smithy.

Descriptive, even affectionate, names are to be found in the day book:

Jefery Heseltine Mrs Sepecttiles Mending	4d
Joseph Coty Bety Key Mending for Chiney Case	4d
Tazey Jack Will Wife Clogs Corkered	7d
Jamey Trouper Jd Wiff Ketel Lid Nop [knob] put on	2d
Bety Sunter Boy Leg iron Mending	2d

Almost all his customers are known by a concoction of parents' names, occupations or personal characteristics, necessary where many had the same names, some with even the same Christian names. We read of Paf Kit Wills, Charley Will Bobs, Thom Sunter Len Thom, Anty Pratt Ruth son. We ourselves remember Fire Sunter, so called because as a boy he once set his bedclothes on fire.

At the end of January, slippery roads brought ten people including Edward Broderick and 'Nedy Postman' to have their horses' shoes sharpened, costing 1s for four shoes. Three horses were also spurned. The first meant the shoe being taken and sharpened all over including the heel, and the spur was a bar fixed across the toe.

By March an occasional mild day heralded better weather, and young Robert Lowes, the son of Robert Lowes, mining agent, brought his minnow net for repair. 'Minert Net Bour Making' — in other words, the hoop on which the net was threaded. This month David fulfilled an order for the Gunnerside joiner and wheelwright, John Calvert, who was building a new stone waggon destined for Arkengarthdale. He supplied parts for the fiddle stick and the shafts, ironwork for the spring pole, hoops for the axletree block and finally hooped the wheels. The total cost was almost £4. On the 22nd April 1872, again joining forces with John Calvert, David wrote 'Pair Wheels and Axletree ironing fit of for Dickey Willey up Dale £2'. Co-operating with other craftsmen, David also supplied loops for coffin handles.

He worked often with Simon Dougill, the builder, who had come to Gunnerside from Pateley Bridge and had three sons, all stonemasons. He made them new *mells* (hammers), a new lime hod, freestone wedges for quarrying work, slate picks and pincers for dressing stone roofing slates, steel chisels, a *trinel* (wheel) for a barrow, twenty cramps for binding masonry, and one day he sharpened for them sixty tools for 1s. Simon's annual bill averaged under £10.

From time to time David repaired all the now-vanished utensils in a dairy: churns, cheese kettles, *chesfords* (cheese vats) and backcans for carrying milk. He was often riveting ears on cans and pails, sometimes putting *beuls* (bowed handles) on frying pans and bakestones (iron girdles for baking oatcake). A comparatively expensive job was *landering* —putting up spouting with elbows, down pipes and screws. In the years under scrutiny he only fitted one range, for Thomas Rutter at Thistlebout 'New Range with Let down Bar 45 lb. 18s. 9d'. In later years, more ranges with his name in raised letters bought from foundries were supplied. As elsewhere in those days the blacksmith substituted for the plumber. Sanitation still meant the 'nessy', and as for central heating it was unheard of. People were inured to cold.

There were then two inns — the Miners Arms and the Kings Head. Isabella Reynoldson at the latter, unmarried and employing a servant girl and a servant lad, was a regular customer and was plainly security-minded. She had a 'Key Altering for Hen Hull [outbuilding]', 'a new Key fiting to Dog Kenel Door Lock', a 'Chaine & Stapel for Pig Hull', besides '2 New teeth for minching machine', a girth put on a barrel, and the handle of a warming pan mended. Isabella had her horse shod and coals fetched for her from Tan Hill.

On the 24th April 1871, David wrote: 'William & family went away with Len Sunter Shandray.' (Leonard Sunter was a miner with five sons, four of whom were also miners.) William had found work as a blacksmith at a colliery in Burnley in Lancashire. The following October 'Elizabeth went with William to Lancashire' where we know she took a job as housekeeper. William did not settle, and after another move he returned to Askrigg in Wensleydale, only six, albeit hilly, miles from Gunnerside. Here he became landlord of the Crown Inn with a blacksmith's shop behind it. Elizabeth then kept house for John until he married and she herself married and went to live at Wetherby.

For the first half of February 1872, David Calvert simply entered in the day book 'Me of[f] Work' and 'Me poorley Soarthroat of[f] Work', but on the 14th February we read 'Me started Work'. By March this was chiefly in the fields 'On getening out muck', 'On trowing out muck', and 'On dressing Muck', and on the 20th March 'On Geting bedin in pasture'. In May 1872 he was ill again and described his condition as 'ME WAS [worse] THAN NOTHING'.

Each year, from April or May onwards when the lambs were beginning to dot the fields until haytime in July, a stock of coal was fetched by horse and cart from Tan Hill and William Gill pits at the head of Arkengarthdale. A page is devoted to these annual pilgrimages. In 1871 he sent various men for loads. A cart held five or six corves at 9d or 1s a corf. Often the cost at the pit was 3s 9d a cartload. Getting peats for fuel is not mentioned in these years, but peat coups were repaired for other Gunnerside people.

Haytime was preceded by a rush to have sheep shears sharpened for clipping at 1s each. A new pair cost 2s. Mowing was heralded by a demand for scythes. Only a few had bought mowing machines in 1871. For the miner/cowkeeper, even if he could afford to pay for one they were not worth the outlay. So David bought in blades and shafts and sold about twenty scythes in 1871. John Coty bought one for 6s, and

Tan Hill coal pit. Coal was mined here at the head of Arkengarthdale in the thirteenth century, and Tan Hill was one of several pits. The poor-quality coal burnt well with peat, and was fetched by horse and cart from miles around. It ceased to be worked in the early 1930s.

Jacky Bell Lad, probably Christopher Bell aged thirteen, a short scythe for 5s 6d. Others required parts: grass nails, wedges and hoops. On the 1st August we read 'Miedeling Jack Scythe altring and hea[l] hoop grass nail mending', and on the 7th August 'Wm Sunter Son Scythe altring Resd [received] tobacco for it'. William was the grocer, draper and postmaster of Gunnerside. But Jeffery Heseltine needed his mowing machine repairing, costing 5d, and David went to Mill Bridge, a good mile up the dale, for Henry Woodward's machine 'to Put it Right 1s'. His own haytime was short-lived. On 17 July 1872 he started 'Moing for Hay' in his field, Corn Close, by the beck side, and he finished on the 23rd.

Whenever there was a lull David was on 'Turning Shoses' [making new horse shoes], and on 30 September 1872 he recorded 'Old man & me turnen Shoes'. David was obviously well thought of for both shoeing and veterinary work. Bleeding was still occasionally practised. 'Cit Rutter going up to house to bleed Gallow foot', (Cit Rutter, a leadminer with a wife and seven children, lived high above Gunnerside at Whins Hall.) Also his green ointment was in demand: 'John Jamey Pratt Box ointment for fole leg 9d'.

David knew the horses which were brought in regularly as well as their masters: Old Charley, Old Peg, Dolphin, Daper, Halfway Charlie. But mostly they were someone's 'Gallow', short for Galloway. James Percival's horse was fractious and James Alderson owned a 'Graite Horse' and a 'Lump knee' one. In February 1871 when a 'Stranger Man' called to have his horse's shoe removed, we sense curiosity at seeing a new face. On New Year's Day, 1872, George Fawcett, known as Simy Dode, must have come down from Angram to have his ass shod. We read: 'Mr Fawcet Schoolmarster Keld Ass Shoeing 9d'. Simy Dode, who was lame, taught at Keld School for very many years and in later life had a very small pony.

Another of David's customers was 'Muker Docktor', Dr Abraham Bowerman Kernot, remembered as a little man who served the dale for some thirty years.[3] He came to Muker straight from training in 1864 and moved to Reeth six years later. For a time he still brought his mare to be shod at Gunnerside, and in 1871 paid a three-year bill for £5 6s 8d for shoeing, frost nails and occasional household repairs.

As time went on there was work for various public bodies — the schools, the highway surveyor, the sanitary committee, the Literary Institute, the pasture committee for whom David made a tar-mark P, and for the surveyor two drags — swinging hurdles fixed across a beck. After making irons for a bell, he was 'on with Bell hanging' for 'Mr Keyworth School Marster'.

Although mining companies usually employed their own smiths, they occasionally ordered small items from David, such as clevises and kibbles (hooks and containers for lead ore fixed on a leather harness worn by a miner). For the Old Gang Company he was 'Up one night Midnight to repair Pump Rod and making shorter', and in September 1880 he was 'One Night Sir Francis to repair steel rod for Donkey Pump'. (The Sir Francis level in Gunnerside Gill was then being driven.) On the 28th July 1871 he made a 'new Bolt for Wheel Arm' for Knowles's woollen mill, which was Haverdale Mill (eventually pulled down).

At Whitaside Mine he earned 3s sometimes 3s 6d a day, but at the smithy with a run on shoeing he might make 10s 6d. He often bought scrap iron, sometimes from the hawker, Joseph Abbot, who always attended sales. The infinitesimal sums paid for small jobs contrast sharply with the kind of prices paid nowadays — 'Maty Jone Sled Chane Mending 2d'. Customarily bills were settled annually — an iniquitous system, for the sudden influx of money often resulted in reckless spending at the inns.

Every now and again he takes a day off to attend sales or funerals — 'ME AT HARDLAKES SALE'. And fairs were always noted — 'ME AT BROUGHFILL BOUGHT GALLOW TRASH' in September 1871 refers to a poor bargain at Brough Hill Fair. In October that year he whitened the smithy in readiness for Gunnerside Fair. This was a farmer's day, but it included stalls and was an important event in local life.

In the early 1870s David does not mention the great Gunnerside Wesleyan festivals, Midsummer day and Shortest Day, which later became occasions for reunions of those people who had left.[4] One of the daughters of David's son, William, Margaret

Gunnerside Fair in the 1890s, with buyers and spectators. The cattle are standing alongside the beck. On the left of the bridge is the Kings Head Inn.

Ann, used to tell us in her old age that in the mid 1870s, then aged eight, she came from Burnley with her father who carried a black tin box over his shoulder, by coach from Skipton to Buckden in Wharfedale. Then they walked the fifteen miles over the Stake Pass via Askrigg to Gunnerside for Midsummer Day. On Cow Hill behind the smithy, spice and milk were dispensed. 'The hillsides were clad wi' people.'

Very occasional trips by horse and shandrey to Reeth or Richmond enlivened the daily routine. Once they saw a circus at Reeth, and in April 1872 David went to meet his sister, Elizabeth, at Buckden on a very snowy day and 'lost his labour'. Nutting and gathering sloes in Ivelet Woods in the autumn were seldom missed.

Margaret and Charlotte had married, the one living at Darlington and the other at Liverpool. Addy, who had always shown a flare for creating bonnets and hats, worked as a milliner in the 1870s at Darlington but eventually in Wakefield. 'The bonnets were beautiful and the hats marvellous.' At Darlington she had felt that she deserved the post of head milliner which meant earnings of £16 a year. Mary, who did not marry, in time returned home and became the mainstay of the family.

Young David eventually took the Joiners Arms and the blacksmith's shop at

David and Margaret Calvert, in a photograph taken when they were visiting their son John in Wales during the 1870s. John, a schoolmaster, moved back to Pease's School in Darlington; he was a keen photographer

Thwaite, and later moved to Buckden and then to Hawes. Another son, William, served part of his time at Richmond and Burnley, and settled at Askrigg as blacksmith and innkeeper at the Crown Inn. He died aged eighty-one in 1926. It was James who carried on both Gunnerside and Thwaite smithies, and when Thwaite was closed, his son, William, continued at Gunnerside up to 1966. The smithy still functions, run by William's son, Jim Calvert, who has successfully adapted to modern needs by taking up plumbing and wrought-iron work.

On Monday the 25th December 1871, David senior wrote in his day book in large script 'Cri Mas day Holaday'. If it was fine on that day, he would see, as he often saw after work, a crowd of men, almost all lead-miners, clustered round the favourite meeting place the bridge. But only twelve years later David, writing to his daughter Mary at Darlington, pictures a new and dire state of affairs: 'All is in a very dull way at present. A good many is gone away and more will have to go yet. Their will be a total stop with the Mines this next month except for a few men the mineing co are obliged to keep on till the lease is up.'[5]

David was now sixty-five. He had finished work or there was no work to do and some friction had arisen with his son, David. At Christmas he thanks Mary for a trunk of good secondhand clothes sent by rail and carrier, probably belonging to a former employer who had died. The clothes included 'one Set of black' which was 'rather too good for a coman man but no wors for that, I shall ware them if I live long enough. The Hats is splendid rather tite but will alter in youseing them.' In return as a New Year's gift he sends Mary a stamp to get 'A Penny worth of Sweets'. In answer to a request for 'aney old Spectacles nocking about' Mary sends two pairs and receives the reply, 'Mother can see very well with one Pair and I can see at a distance with the other Pair.'

Nonetheless they are very busy adding on to the house in anticipation of Mary's return, and enduring cold and discomfort in the meantime. 'Mother is set up with the Sitting Room Fireplace its a nice Plain substanshal one no fancy emages about it.' David and his wife, facing a bleak future, were helped out in old age by their children who had found economic salvation by self-help.

1   Based on David Calvert's Day Book for 1871 and 1872 lent by Mr Calvert Chapman (1892—1975), also the recollections of Miss M A Calvert (1867—1953), Mrs M Waudby, Miss J Calvert and Mr J Calvert.

2   PRO RG10/4872 Enumerated census Gunnerside 1871.

3   NYCRO, ZLB, Dr Kernot's Case Books 1867—1875. Also *Darlington and Stockton Times* (2 March 1895), obituary, and *Medical Register* (1890) and *Medical Directory* (1890). Dr Kernot was MRCSE and licentiate of the Society of Apothecaries. He moved from Muker to Reeth following the death of Dr McCollah, and married Sarah Hillary of Fremington late in life. She died after the birth of a son. He took a prominent part in Reeth institutions and it was he who commented to the Garths on the improvement in the cattle noted during his long sojourn in the dale. He died in 1895.

4   For the origin of the festivals, see M Batty's *Gunnerside Chapel and Gunnerside Folk* (1967), and for recollections 'Stories of Swaledale', a series of four articles written by John Bell for the *Darlington and Stockton Times* in 1938.

5   Letters written by David Calvert to his eldest daughter, Mary, from December 1883 to March 1885, lent by Mr J Calvert.

The Gamekeeper

Harry Roger Storey kept a diary from the 1st January 1898, when he was sixteen, until the 18th August 1955, a month before his death at the age of seventy-three. He made daily entries in a neat small hand always ending with a brief note on the weather in a series of printed pocket diaries.[1] Over the years the entries reflect events and changing times, for Harry lived through three wars, and saw the arrival of the gramophone, wireless, electricity, the cinema, popular photography, the substitution of the telegram by the telephone, and the general use of the bicycle, the motor bus and above all the motor car, all of which affected him personally.

He was born in the house next to the church at Castle Bolton in Wensleydale. His grandfather had been a builder, and had run the pottery using local clay in Church Lane, Redmire, where red roofing and drainage tiles, bricks and flower pots were made. When his father James Storey was fourteen, the grandfather died, and James carried on the pottery with his mother for a time, until he was appointed an underkeeper on Lord Bolton's estate.

In 1894 James started as head keeper for the Vyners of Newby Hall near Ripon for the grouse shooting on Askrigg Moor and the adjacent Crackpot and Muker Edge in Swaledale. He moved with his family to the Warren, an isolated house situated at a sharp bend of the road between Carperby and Askrigg. Here, as well as his work as keeper, he had charge of a famous warren of silver-grey rabbits formerly belonging to the Metcalfes of Nappa Hall, from whom the Vyners had indirectly inherited it and a small estate by marriage. The house dates from 1757 when it was then rebuilt as a house for the warrener.[2] A wall, in parts eight feet high, built of limestone, circles from the house, enclosing the seventy-five acres of the warren. Originally this was 100 acres before the railway track, now cutting off the warren from the River Ure, was laid on the south side. A central feature is a drumlin, then bracken-covered, known as Lady Hill, topped by a group of windswept Scots pines, still a noted landmark. In the diaries it is always referred to as the *Plump*, a dialect word for a clump of trees.

At the Warren, James and his wife brought up eight children — two died in infancy — five girls and three boys, of whom Harry was the eldest. It was a close and happy family life, especially before the children grew up and married. James

The Warren at the present day. It was built in 1757. Hawbank forms the background.

kept one or two cows, a pig or two, hens, a pony called Jenny and a trap, a mare called Fanny and a cart, several dogs, and ferrets. A seed and a ploughing field grew grass for hay and turnips with which to feed the rabbits in winter.

The origin of the silver-greys is not clear, but in 1794 they were 'said to have been brought some years since from a warren in Lincolnshire whither they had been brought from Ireland'.[3] The warren may well have been established by Thomas Metcalfe of Nappa Hall (1687—1756), who had entered into a bond not to part with any alive.[4] In those days the valuable fur, used for trimming, was exported to Russia and China 'to be worn by the principal people'. The silver-greys were larger than wild rabbits and bred less frequently — a characteristic of warren rabbits. Their close black fur with white hairs shone like silver in the sun. Also — shades of General Woundwort in *Watership Down* — they were aggressive, chasing intruders, whether rabbits or hares, from burrow to burrow until they killed them, and even at times intimidating stoats. In snowstorms drifts had to be dug away from the walls lest they escape.

The rabbits were caught for sale both dead and alive in November, December and January. On moonlight nights they were either driven into nets, fifty yards long by a yard high, or trapped in *types*, of which there were five, four oblong and one round, near different walls of the warren. These were deep walled pits, the round one six feet in diameter. Across each was fixed a long, narrow wooden box with

The Plump in the rabbit warren.

open ends leading to a *smout* (small hole) in the wall . The bottom of the box had two pivoting boards so that rabbits entering from either end were tipped into the pit.[5]

In the late nineteenth century Harry records catching annually some 200 couple and, after paunching and skinning, despatching them to game dealers. Carcases could be sent in hampers to London by the 7pm train and be in cold storage by 4am. Many, mostly alive, were bought by the game dealer, F S Graham of Aysgarth, for 2s each. Some went to stock burrows in other parts of the country and a few went to America. The fur became fashionable as a lining for tweed motor coats, and King Edward VII sent one of these handsome garments to the Tsar of Russia, Nicholas II.[6] But in the end imitation fur destroyed this side of the trade. In 1922 when the Storeys left and later when myxomatosis spread in the 1950s, what was probably the last warren of silver-greys in the country faded out.

When the diaries begin, besides attending to the rabbits, Harry's activities were mostly centred round home, with his duties as gamekeeper limited to the August and September shoots. He looks after the dogs, and is constantly going off on errands for a gun licence, yeast or taking letters to post to nearby villages. Always armed with a gun and looking at traps, he was out daily. Often he went up Hawbank, a steep hillside clothed with ancient woodland on the north side of the Warren, from there to a vast open pasture above it, Oxclose, to the Foxholes, and beyond to the hill called Ellerkin, and beyond that to the millstone grit outcrop, the Greets.

Hawbank was famous for hazelnuts, and the Storeys also picked brambles there, and collected fire sticks, pea rods and saplings for making walking sticks. Going 'a-nutting' crops up in the diaries, and again and again in records of the Dales. In the 1840s, hazelnuts were plentiful enough to be offered for sale in Hawes.

When Harry began work he was one of three underkeepers for the Vyners, one of whom, Jim Hutchinson, always spoken of as 'Hutch', lived at Rash in upper Swaledale, and in 1902 he married Harry's sister, Alice, thus forging a link with that dale. His was a solitary but not a lonely job. He enjoyed membership of a large family, the fraternity of keepers and, throughout his life, a good relationship with the 'gentlemen', his employers. In this age his wage, although comparable with that for other work, seems minute — £1 a week for an underkeeper, and, in 1918, £1 15s with a cottage, rates and a suit provided each year. A firm at Ripon, Jacksons, made up the cloth, and a member of the family, George Jackson, artist and play-wright, was a close friend. No doubt the wage was supplemented in several ways, not least by living off the land, and as Richard Jefferies says: 'The gamekeeper is one of those fortunate individuals whom all the world tips.' By and large his pleasures were independent of money. Relatives, with whom he stayed for holidays, lived in diverse places.

Goods, too, were cheap. In 1905 he bought boots for 14s a pair and a suit for 25s. In 1916 another suit cost £4 10s and an overcoat from Burberrys 45s, but by 1920 he was paying £4 4s 9d for an overcoat and £3 for strong boots. In 1926 a piano cost him £35, and shortly after a bicycle for his daughter 50s, although in 1902 he had paid £6 15s for a 'free wheel bike' for himself.

By 1904 Harry's prowess at shooting and fishing had obviously improved. He shot, rabbits, pigeons, jackdaws, snipe, hawks, a *grayback* (hooded crow), an occasional dipper, an owl, a *heronsew* (heron) and cats which were unwelcome in the warren. Cats, too, were skinned and their pelts cured. Once a white weasel is similarly treated. He himself stuffed a fox's head. Once he saw a goosander by the river. One morning he was up at 3.30am to fish, and he visited Hawes to be taught to tie flies, probably by James Blades (Sproats), a famous fisherman. In 1906 he bought a rod for 10s 6d, but later made his own and some for other people from split cane or greenheart. On two long day's fishing in upper Swaledale, he and a companion caught seventy-eight trout, and in September 1902 he and George Collier, the other underkeeper, caught 400 crayfish using liver as bait, and sent them to the Vyners.

The occasional otter and frequent fox hunts, the latter led by Squire Tomlinson of Aysgarth, master of the Wensleydale Hounds, were then part of his life. Fox tracing and trapping in order to have a bagged fox for the hunt was then a common practice. Sometimes a cleft in a crag was utilised as a trap, a stone *kist*, but more often the kist was a narrow oak box about three feet six inches long. The fox unwittingly entered a trapdoor at one end and at the other, in trying to get out, it bit a stick lightly attached to iron bars and let the trapdoor down. On the 19th March

1900 we read: 'A cover of six inch of snow. Met [two other keepers] on Oxclose traced a fox ... on the edge of Greets ... and holed it ... dug it out and took it over to Squires.' Five days later, 'Went over to Squires to turn the fox down at Aysgarth chased the fox the high side of Thornton Rust round Addlebrough and holed in Whitfield.'

Beside sending game and crayfish to the Vyners, plovers' eggs, collected and hardboiled in the spring, were despatched. On the 31st March 1904 he 'Got a Pickling tank for Plovers eggs from York', and that same year sent off 228 eggs in four batches. When the Protection of Lapwings Act was passed in 1928, this ceased. Instead, the eggs of black-headed gulls which nest on the shores of Summer Lodge Tarn were sometimes collected. The Storeys had a stuffed black-headed gull dating from their arrival in Wensleydale in the 1880s.

The doctors who lived at Aysgarth figure from time to time as sportsmen shooting pheasants with the gamekeeper, as the recipients of gifts of game, as well as in their professional roles. On one occasion we read: 'Father cut his foot with an axe. Dr Hime came and sawed [sewed] it up.' Harry himself was prone to severe colds. In May 1904 the death of little Tom, one of the children of his sister, Alice, who was brought to the Warren for an operation, is a poignant entry, recording an illness in an era without easy access to hospitals or surgical treatment.

Quite early on Harry had taken on the burden of putting down usually old animals, from horses to dogs, by shooting them in a district without a veterinary surgeon at hand. But once he wrote 'shot old Mettle in a mistake', and next day he buried her in a grave on Hawbank.

Dogs continually appear in the diary. He trains them, sells pups, meets new dogs at the station, buys biscuits for them — setters, retrievers, spaniels, labradors named Gip, Beaut, Prince, Bess, Rover, Sweep, Don, Nigger. On the 29th January 1938 he wrote: 'John Banks came up with his dog. It had swallowed a sock. We gave it lard and washing soda and got it to vomit it up again.' Help to relatives, friends and neighbours pervaded life in those days.

A striking aspect of Harry's life was its mobility. As a young man, after walking miles during the day, he had energy to set off at night to the then numerous village events. If he stayed late, usually at balls ('champion stirs') until four or five o'clock in the morning, he sometimes stopped overnight with a relative. On both work and pleasure he was often away from home. As early as 1898 a new bicycle, except for hilly journeys, was preferred to the pony, and, although he never owned a motor car, mobility continued throughout his life, partly because gamekeeper's work took him to other parts of the country, partly because his youngest brother, Jack, started a garage in Askrigg, thus giving access to cars, and partly because of his sociable nature. His infectious enjoyment and ready smile must have brightened many an outing.

In the early years he played football, sometimes on Christmas Day, then a two

Carperby Feast, circa 1900, with the Bainbridge brass band in the foreground.

day holiday with Boxing Day; he attended what was then a big gathering in Swaledale, the Whitaside sheep-washing, when dinner was provided by the Charlesworths of Grinton shooting lodge, sheep-clipping at Nappa Hall, fairs for the sale of stock, Muker Show without fail, and shepherds' dinners at Askrigg, Muker and Keld Green. The gamekeeper was closely involved with these last events on behalf of his employer, issuing invitations and paying for the dinners — in 1910, £5 for about forty men. In different years Muker, Keld and Gunnerside bands, walking over from Swaledale, came round at the Christmas season.

Harry attended every nearby village feast. He won a copper kettle for shooting at Carperby Feast in 1905. There were concerts, the occasional circus, a wild beast show at Askrigg and Wombwell's menageries at Leyburn. Accompanied by friends on their bicycles, he visited local sights and ruins, once going to Ilkley and Bolton Abbey. On the 22nd May 1901 he writes: 'Rode down to Redmire to see the stang riding came back about 11.30.' This was perhaps the last performance in the dale of the custom of parading an effigy of a man or woman, who had misbehaved, through the village street with an accompaniment of beating drums, tin cans, and the recitation of a rhyme. In that same year he had begun to meet Nell Hunter, a girl from Cragg Hall Farm between Thwaite and Keld in Swaledale. 'Sister Alice & I ... went to Muker to the Reading room ball a right jolly stir broke up about 3 went up to

Thwaite with N.' On the 14th September 1904 'myself and N.H. and two friends went with the train to Morecambe'. They were there by 9am and reached home about midnight.

Either marathon trips or short journeys from place to place in the dale by train were possible in those days of the railway. On the 25th June 1904, the day of the Hardraw Scar band contest, he wrote: 'Rode bike up to Askrigg took train from Askrigg to Hawes. Went over to the Scar very few people there [because it was a poor day] came back with the 8.40 trip.' For a week round Christmas 1899 he and his brother, Jim, going by train, stayed with relations at Burnley, and visited Briarfield, both towns to which the families of leadminers had gone from Swaledale. The visit, including three theatres, was fun, but there is no doubt that had the sisters kept diaries they would have had much duller stay-at-home lives to record.

When Harry was twenty-seven his father had retired, and the Vyners, who had rented the shooting rights since 1884 at £30 a year, gave up. They had failed in their appeal against a new assessment of £400 a year. He was engaged as gamekeeper for Askrigg Moor by J E Riley of Arden Hall, Accrington, Lancashire, who leased the shooting rights relinquished by the Vyners. It was a turning point in his career. After nine years courting he felt able to marry, and he found a house, Sunnybank, up the moor road at Askrigg. On the 7th April 1910 he and Nell Hunter were married at Muker Church. His employer gave him £4 as a wedding present.

But Mr Riley died, and new men formed a syndicate, amongst whom was W E Farrer from Greyrigg, near Kendal, who remained a member for thirty-seven years. Later, another member was Sir Raymond Evershed, the Master of the Rolls. Some of these had shoots elsewhere, so that Harry was at times far afield at Gatehouse of Fleet in Kirkcudbrightshire shooting pheasants and wild duck, or at Holker Hall, and on many local shoots.

His fishing continued, with some fox tracing. He became an authority on flies, tying his own: Waterhen, Winter Brown, Crimson Partridge, Spring Black. On the 16th May 1932 he landed a 2lb 5oz trout and won a fishing reel for the second biggest fish caught that year. His leather pannier with an embossed lid is kept as a memento in the family.

Most days now Harry systematically covered different parts of the moor. It is plain from the diary that rain and cold were preferable to heat when the sun beat mercilessly down. Light snow was no obstacle, but in 1947 he was prevented from reaching the moor by the storm beginning on the 2nd February and lasting until the 23rd March.

An area of some 2,000 acres, Askrigg Moor rises up to 1,850 feet above sea level. Two roads run over it, one to Muker and one to Reeth, and, linking them, one of the gamekeeper's tracks crosses Green Mea, frequently mentioned in the diary. Other 'trods' lead to Summer Lodge Tarn, threading ways between peat hags, all routes invisible to the stranger except for here and there the telltale imprint of a boot on soft ground. In the early years Beezy Hut, now demolished, on the site of Beezy leadmine, and Greets Hut were in use, but as time passed Stackhill House on the west of the Muker road became the place for shelter and rendezvous. Here a spring supplies water and a few trees make it a landmark.

The keeper's keen eye roving over his territory noticed at once the slightest change. In the spring grouse droppings indicated the number of birds. Plover and curlew returned to the moor drew attention to predators by mobbing. Harry was on the look-out for nests, and his diary records the start of the breeding season. On the 1st April 1915 he 'found first plover's nest'; 10th April 1905, 'saw first young rabbit in the warren'; 1st May 1923, 'found first grouse nest with eggs in'; 11th May 1907, 'first young grouse seen on Askrigg Moor'; 27th April 1900, 'Heard cuckoo first time'; but on the 16th May he 'caught a cuckoo'.

There was no mercy in the cause of preserving the game. Traps were sometimes fixed at the top of a pole. Poisoned eggs, rabbits and rats were put down, hung in trees or pushed into walls. He catches weasels, stoats and crows. On the 19th May 1920 he 'waited of the carrion coming on to the nest, waited 4½ hours Shot the old hen', and on the 16th December 'shot a Bustard hawk'. On the 27th May 1921

Stackhill House in winter.

Harry Storey burning heather on Askrigg Moor.

'searching awhile for merlin Hawk's nest ... shot the cock and put a trap for the hen', and three days later caught it. Every year a vermin list was sent to his employers. That for 1920 read: '48 stoats, 17 weasels, 12 hawks, 14 carrion crows, 5 magpies, 12 hedgehogs, 15 gulls, 12 crows, 2 cats, 3 foxes, 1 raven'.

Early in the year he burnt areas of heather with helpers who were paid. Hutch, alerted by telegram, often joined him. Sometimes they were both 'guttering' to lead water from boggy places, and always in June repairing butts and sometimes building new ones. He is also cleaning up in general, whitewashing the shooting hut and boundary stones, buying calico which Nell makes up into beaters' flags, carting up coal and drink to the hut, and later presenting sprigs of white heather to his friends.

Each year at the end of June, often with a companion or the policeman, he kept watch as the gypsies and potters began to assemble in their caravans for Askrigg Hill

Fair, held on a huge pasture adjoining the moor. As the day of the fair approached, he was keeping vigil all night. On a vigil in 1903, they spotted a stray cur dog which had been worrying sheep, and followed it for miles to Whitaside Moor, where more men joined in the hunt until one of them shot it. But by the end of the First World War this was no longer necessary, as the once-crowded hill fair had all but faded out. On the whole, poaching in his day did not pose a problem. Occasionally one or two local men were cautioned for collecting plovers' eggs, for catching rabbits or for shooting grouse.

All this activity led up to the 'Glorious Twelfth'. In 1898 the Vyners and their party arrived by train, and stayed at the King's Arms Hotel in Askrigg. A number of horses were hired from farmers for transport up the very steep mile to the moor, and that year he took Jenny for Lord Londonderry to ride up on. A waggon and horse brought food, and other horses wore panniers in which the grouse were collected. On the Twelfth 1898 they shot '327½ brace of grouse, 2 brace of Golden Plover, 1 snipe, 1 hare — a very fine day'. Next day at Crackpot and Muker Edge it was 238 brace of grouse, 1 brace of snipe and 1½ brace of plover. On the 16th the party left, but returned on the 12th September for another two days' sport. This was the regular pattern. In 1903, the Vyners came by motor car.

Each year the bags recorded in the keeper's game-book varied, sometimes because the broods had been affected by cold, wet springs, and sometimes because the birds were stricken with disease, as in 1918 and 1925. On the 13th August 1901, Harry comments: 'A beautiful show of birds', and in 1934 'a good show of birds strong on the wing and in big packs'. But in 1925 there was a poor show, especially at the west end of the moor. He states that the record bag for Askrigg Moor in one day was 565 brace in 1902. In his father's day in 1896 the best bag for the whole season was 1,783 brace. In that year 1,190 'went to market'. In those years there were usually a few blackcock amongst the bag, and in 1920 a 'ringed dotteral' [plover]. Besides those sold, many were sent as gifts to the Vyners' friends and relatives. Others were distributed locally to the station masters, the policeman, the vicar, farmers who had sheep rights on the moor and others. In 1902, a particularly good year, 211 were so disposed of. In 1905 the shoot cost £718 3s 2d, of which £276 5s 2d was keepers' wages, £66 18s horses and beaters etc, and £375 (sic) the rent of Askrigg Moor.

One alarming experience occurred in July 1925 when a fire broke out near the summit of the moor off the Reeth road. Starting so close to the shooting season, Harry and helpers and even the owners of the shooting rights hurried to the scene. They trenched all round the fire to contain it, carried water with the aid of a horse, and stayed there for two whole days and nights. After feverish activity they won through, and all that remained was to view the damage and pay forty-four men different sums at the rate of 10s for a day or a night.

However, Harry wrote of the following season: 'During nesting and hatching the weather was very favourable, the grouse nested well 8 to 10 eggs, they hatched off well and no signs of any disease.' (Strangely, nests on burnt ground are more difficult to find than elsewhere.) The total bag that year was 1,090½ brace of grouse, of which 696½ were from Askrigg Moor. As time went on, in line with experience elsewhere on other moors, the bags diminished.

Given its sporting character, what a richly happy life it was! Day after day spent in the open air, often away to the moors with all that offered of freedom and the constant interest of wildlife, albeit sacrificed by shooting and trapping to the preservation of the game. His hobbies were many, including gardening, dressing walking sticks, tying flies, making anything, and as early as 1908 taking photographs.

Home life was consistently a partnership. From her Swaledale upbringing Nellie inherited traditional practices: making feather beds, stobbed rugs and quilts; and she always knitted with a knitting stick tucked into a belt. The house was kept in perfect order. In 1913 Harry bought a phonograph and the next year an organ at a sale. Under the window of a front room stood his father's desk, an oak box on long legs once used at the Warren for the rabbit accounts. On the 25th January 1915 a baby — to be their only child — was born. Besides summoning the doctor and welcoming a nurse he comments: 'A splendid day a daughter Nellie and baby doing well'.

Meanwhile, the outbreak of war in August 1914 coincided with the preparation for grouse shooting, and for four days the diary is neglected. Eventually we learn of Belgian refugees arriving and other items of war news. Harry himself, aged thirty-two, was at first rejected for the army, and that year he organised the fencing of the boundary between Wensleydale and Swaledale on Askrigg Moor with posts and rails. However, two years later he was passed fit and joined up as a gunner in the Royal Horse and Royal Field Artillery. He served in France, mercifully surviving. In January 1919 his captain gave him a statement, meant as a recommendation for civilian employment, that he was 'sober, very steady and hard working, and reliable, a valuable man'. But it was hardly necessary. On the 17th February he wrote, 'Started work at my old job'.

Over the fifty odd years covered by the diaries, entries record national events from the relief of Pretoria to the end of the Second World War. Other entries recall deaths and accidents, sometimes on the moor, and one in particular would have saddened him. On the the 7th June 1930, Richard Trotter, with whom he and Nellie had often obtained a lift in his butcher's trap to Swaledale, was thrown from his horse and later died.

In 1924 the Storeys moved to a larger house, Prospect House next to Sunnybank, and were soon taking in visitors, often personal friends, and putting up beaters in August. Birthday parties for Margaret marked the passage of the years. Harry made her a little wooden bed and a doll's house, also 'twilting' (quilting) frames for friends. In 1927, coming late to church-going, he was confirmed, and was soon elected to

Nellie Storey in 1965.

Harry Storey and Tiger checking nests on Askrigg Moor in the 1940s.

the church council and made a churchwarden. It was a token of the respect in which he was held by the community.

Most of the village events — the feasts and the balls — had faded away. Instead they went to whist drives and dances and on British Legion trips by charabanc. As early as the 1920s they had been going long journeys by motor car — to the Lake District, Whitby and Scarborough — and in these years the newly-started bus service began to compete with the train for custom. One or another of them spent holidays in London, Edinburgh and Scotland. They had long ago heard a friend's

*Harry Storey and Tiger with Ella Pontefract
at Stackhill House, 1941.*

gramophone and were now listening to the wireless. Christmas after Christmas, invitations and return invitations for friends, including us, followed the same pattern, except that by this time the brass bands no longer came over from Swaledale.

On the 2nd September 1939, Margaret Storey and James Scarr, a farmer of Coleby Hall, a mile from Askrigg, were married and had their honeymoon cut short by the outbreak of war. Immediately evacuees arrived, the military occupied Stackhill House and the Home Guard Greets Hut, and Harry enrolled as a special constable. In time the arrival of grandchildren brought a new interest.

Although the dates for shooting became very erratic and 1944 turned out to be a very poor year, Harry's work as gamekeeper continued through the war and the 1940s. In 1952 he retired, and the last entry in the diaries is for the 18th August 1955: 'A dull showery day. Had a good night. Got up about 10, had a walk with the dog.' He died on the 13th September. For some days Nellie tried to keep up the entries. But forty-five years of loving partnership had ended.

1   Based on the diaries of Harry Storey, gamekeeper, kept from January 1898 to August 1955, lent to us by Mrs J Scarr.
2   NYCRO ZB 1400. Alexander Fothergill's Diary, 21st February 1757.
3   Tuke, *General View of Agriculture of the North Riding*, 1794, p 70.
4   NYCRO ZB 1400. Alexander Fothergill's Diary, 12th December 1774.
5   Shown to us by Mr F T Dinsdale.
6   Recollections of Mr J Storey, Harry's youngest brother.

The Hamlets of Birkdale and Raven Seat

HOLLOW MILL CROSS TO CROOK SEAT

The names Birkdale and Raven Seat conjure up the blue distant hills and brown extensive moorlands of the highest lands of the Yorkshire Dales. Not only are the headwaters of the Swale grand, wild and beautiful, but the amphitheatre of fells which encompasses these hamlets has the distinction of being unique in the landscape of the British Isles. A nine-mile circle of hills, all well over 2,000 feet above sea level, begins on the south with Great Shunnor Fell, and continues to Hugh Seat Morville and on to High Seat. (On the other side of the watershed is Mallerstang and the beginnings of the River Eden in Westmorland.) Then dropping down northwards by Fells End to Tailbrigg, the range turns to cross the pass from Swaledale to Westmorland, at 1,698 feet above sea level at Hollow Mill Cross, and rises up again to Coldbergh Edge, to White Mossy Hill and Nine Standards Rigg, just over the county boundary.

In this vast wilderness, the waters of the Swale start in bubbling trickles deep in the bogs of Uldale Gill on Lodge Hags, a flank of High Seat. They flow down Birkdale (or Birtle as it is called locally) as Birkdale Beck, draining both sides of the dale by the gleaming waters of a score or more of sikes, of which the largest are Little and Great Sleddale on the south side, themselves fed by many other rivulets. Great Sleddale Beck thrusts deeply into the hills and its first tributary on Hugh Seat Morville was 'as some say Swale Head'. But usage has firmly established that where Great Sleddale and Birkdale Becks meet, the River Swale begins. It is an important junction, as we shall see. Soon after this meeting on the north side of Birkdale, Whitsundale Beck, again a mighty complex of sikes, joins in, rising on the northern watershed where continuous moorland reaches out to Stainmore. Situated near a loop of its waters in a green hospitable niche of valley floor at 1,300 feet above sea level is Raven Seat, now two farms.

So extensive and so apparently devoid of any traces of man, of trees, or of walls are these moors that it is surprising to learn that they were formerly sought out for their mineral wealth — lead, copper, coal and stone — and that they are also well-used or, more accurately, well-stocked. Although mining and quarrying have gone,

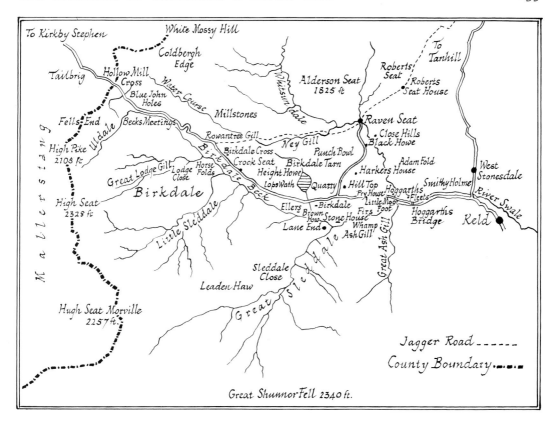

a close look reveals innumerable sheep dotting the fells, sheepfolds, shepherds' huts, and, down by the beck, green pastures, round sheep folds, wash folds by waterfalls, and a plume of smoke from a farmhouse chimney. The lower reaches of Birkdale offer enough reasonably level land for habitation.

For this is sheep country, and the moorlands look well-kept cropped close by sheep. In the whole area including Great Sleddale, where farms round Angram between Keld and Thwaite have pasturage, are grazing some 4,000 Swaledale ewes. Nor does this include lambs or hoggs (young sheep before their first shearing). Each farm has a specific number tied to it, roughly from 100 to 500.

Although we see no walls, there are the invisible boundaries of the heafs or heughs which usually accommodate about 100 sheep, a convenient number for gathering or foddering. A farm may have one, or the largest, four heafs, some apart, some adjacent, and they take their names from the territory, so that the sheep are spoken of as Coldberghers or Uldalers. If a sheep strays from its heaf, which seldom happens, it may become lost and wander for miles across the fells until, recognised by its mark, it is found and returned.

Raven Seat. Note the packhorse bridge in the centre left.

The whole great landscape, sometimes secretive veiled in mist, sometimes expansive warmed by the sun, sometimes prostrated by snow, wind and rain, makes a dramatic setting for the destinies of the past and present inhabitants. Place-names hint at the first dwellers. In the tenth century a Norseman, Hrafn, may have established a summer pasture farm at Raven Seat, and Crook Seat, formerly a house but now a barn, as we shall see, may have early origins. Many field names ending with dale (Old Norse *dalr*) demonstrate the prolonged Norse influence: Nandale, Bobledale, Meanedale and many others. Hugh Seat Morville takes it name from Hugh de Morville who held Pendragon Castle in Mallerstang, and who in 1170 was one of the knights involved in the murder of Thomas à Becket. Later on Lady Anne Clifford, Countess of Pembroke, Dorset and Montgomery, whose castles included Pendragon, had a pillar inscribed A P 1664, still to be seen, put on this summit as a boundary stone for her Mallerstang property.

The hill, Robert's Seat above Raven Seat, must take its name from 'Roberto de Raynsate' who paid a fifteenth tax on his goods in 1301[1], and a mile east of this is Alderson Seat, perpetuating in its name the predominant clan in medieval upper Swaledale. As we saw in Oxnop, from the thirteenth century to the Dissolution of the Monasteries, Rievaulx Abbey owned the great pasture in the high dale which became the manor of Muker, of which Oxnop and Birkdale are a part. Until recently the names Alderson, Harker and Metcalfe dominated in a region where newcomers were few.

Little glimpses of happenings in the past crop up. In 1615 Robert Willance of Richmond, who gave his name to Willance Leap and who came from Westmorland, left £100 in his will to his illegitimate daughter, Elizabeth, who was the wife of Giles Alderson of Raven Seat. It was a great deal of money.

Personal names continued to be given to features of the land throughout the centuries. Who was Jenny Whalley who gave her name to a waterfall at Raven Seat? The name of Parrington Currack above Coldbergh Edge is a recent addition. A Parrington came from Dent in the 1840s to work as a farm labourer in Birkdale, and a descendant used this place for organising beaters on grouse-shooting days.

In early years birch forests, the wildwood, provided habitat for deer and other beasts and game. Hunting and hawking were the sports pursued. Thomas Wharton was a tenant of the monks in Birkdale, and after the Dissolution this family, whose estates in Westmorland adjoined upper Swaledale, were granted the manor of Muker. Only tradition relates that Philip Lord Wharton had a lodge of some kind in Birkdale, but it is well authenticated that the Whartons valued the deer and employed keepers for them.[2] In the first years of the seventeenth century, Camden wrote of the other side of the watershed where the Eden rises: 'And in this Tract be safe harbors for Goates and Deere, as well red as fallow, which for their huge bigness with their ragged and branching horns are most sightly.'

On the 29th October 1704, Lord Wharton wrote to his steward, Matthew Smales: 'I am very apt to believe that the red deere in Swaledale are not well looked after. I wish you would tell me which way effectually to mend it.' According to Whitaker, this was the last refuge of the deer 'which remained in considerable numbers northward from Muker as late as the year 1725 ... With the deer vanished their ancient refuge and browse, the woods were gradually consumed by the [lead] smelt mills; for after the warm and sheltered gills were stripped of their clothing, the stags pined for want of their accustomed winter food, of which many died while the rest fell an easy prey to poachers.' Whitaker goes on to say that as deer hunting and hawking ceased, grouse-shooting began, and these are now valuable grouse moors where only foxes and an occasional badger survive.

Starting at the head of the dale on the summit of the pass from Keld to Kirkby Stephen, we leave the magnificent view of Westmorland (now Cumbria), and for five miles descend on a tarred road open to the moorlands. Almost immediately a heap of stones, Hollow Mill Cross, on the north side of the road marks the county boundary (as do two small inscribed stone pillars). It is comparable as an ancient boundary mark with the Rey Cross on Stainmore, but here all signs of the cross have gone.

Except on a summer's day when walkers and motorists cross the pass, only the

Birkdale farmhouse on the right. Above it, by the channel of Great Sleddale Beck, are the ruins of the buildings of Lane End mine, and on the far left is Stone House. On the left of the barn near Birkdale farmhouse can be seen the rounded shape of Brown Howe, and left of that is the field Little Dales, with the foundations of the chapel.

occasional farmer and a parked Land Rover are to be seen. It may be lonely, but over the centuries a host of people have come this way — Norsemen from the west, and Scots raiders bent on pillage. A number of tales of Scots' raiders have been handed down — that Raven Seat was an outpost for giving warning, that the Nine Standards simulated men guarding the boundary, that Brown How, a drumlin below the farmhouse, Birkdale, was the burial place of many after a battle. The persistence of these tales, although unsubstantiated, points to the alarms of the fourteenth century when Pendragon Castle was burnt down and, in lower Swaledale, Ellerton Abbey was pillaged.

Drovers with sheep and cattle passed to and fro, especially in the autumn at the time of Brough Hill Fair. Packhorse gangs came by and those purveyors of news and gossip — the packmen — passed on their regular rounds. Servants walked over from their homes to places of work, and farmers bound for Kirkby Stephen markets and fairs. This Westmorland market town was as near as Hawes in Wensleydale. Some journeying in winter and on foot occasionally lost their way and their lives. On the 23rd November 1641 'Essabel Scaife, daughter of Bartholomew Scaife of Crosby Garret in Westm'land who by travelling over the moores by the Tempestuousness of the weather was perished and Dyed.'[3] Another of these benighted travellers is said to have been frozen upright in a peat bog. It was a not unlikely fate in winter.

On the 24th March 1664 a packman, John Smith, who collected knitted stockings, set off for Westmorland from Swaledale and was never seen again. One James Hutchinson of Hartley, near Kirkby Stephen, the real murderer, accused James Alderson and his two sons of Thwaite of the deed. He described how he saw a corpse in a water hole near Hollow Mill Cross, and also how he was haunted by the apparition of a man 'in a sad-coloured coat and a poake tied about his shoulder and a staffe in his hand'. 106 people, of which 33 were Aldersons, signed a statement vouching for the good names of the accused and the case was dropped.[4] This grim event is perpetuated in the name Blue John Holes near the boundary, a series of limestone shakeholes culminating in one with a deep pool where Duker Beck disappears into rocky depths. Without doubt Blue John was the nickname of the packman whose goods at that date would be predominantly blue. A now delightful place, it is flanked by a sheep-bitten rowan tree and prinked out with flowers associated with lower ground. Its earlier name mentioned by one of the witnesses in the trial, Helen Alderson, seems to have been Hawkinge Bower, a name evocative of the peregrines once common in these high places.

Birkdale was not too remote for nonconformity to take root. It is hinted that the packman wearing his sad-coloured coat was a Quaker. In 1670 Simon Harker of Birkdale was present at a meeting of Quakers held at the house of Elizabeth Cherry at Kearton, ten or eleven miles down the dale, and for his attendance in lieu of a fine he had a brass pot distrained worth 7s. Simon died three years later and was buried in 'his own Ground Birkdale'.[5]

Duker Beck surfaces near Becks Meetings, where a shepherd's hut and sheepfolds on a patch of open ground make a landmark. Above on the north, at the south-eastern end of Coldbergh Edge, may be seen a currack named Millstones. Signs of quarrying are obvious here, and comparatively recently the gritstone was utilised for quoins for house and barn building. Coldbergh is well named. When the wind beats against it, blown spray funnels off like the smoke from a fire.

Also near the boundary starts a four-mile long water race designed to feed Birkdale Tarn lower down, formerly a small natural tarn, now eleven acres, for the use of water to drive water wheels and engines for pumping water from Lane End and Little Moor Foot leadmines below it. Such watercourses were not unique and it resembles that in Oxnop Gill, but is much longer. It was a tremendous undertaking, cut by hand probably in the early nineteenth century. 1757 seems too early a date, but in that year a Richard Alderson of Birkdale was paid £7 13s 11d for damage to his ground by watercourses.[6] The race starts at Uldale Gill at 1,650 feet above sea level, proceeds north-west, crosses the pass just below the pillar inscribed Nateby, travels north to circumvent Duker Beck, then takes a direct course along Coldbergh Side following the 1,625 contour, tapping many becks, circles Height Howe on its north side and enters the northernmost point of the tarn at 1,600 feet above sea level. It is visible here and there as a channel in the grass, but it was wide enough once to be marked in blue on Ordnance Survey maps (see the 2½ins sheet 35/80).

Continuing down the dale, our road takes a sharp bend at Rowantree Gill, at which point a road formerly debouched directly for Raven Seat, dropping down alongside Ney Gill, a tributary of Whitsundale Beck. Although remembered and marked as a footpath on maps, it is one of many moorland roads lost through disuse. In 1788 the inhabitants of Birkdale were indicted at quarter sessions for not keeping it in repair 'to the great damage and nuisance of all . . .' It was described as eight yards wide and as 'a certain common and ancient highway leading from the market town of Kirkby Stephen ... towards the village of Raven Seat ... for all the liege subjects of our lord the King ... on horseback or on foot ... and to drive their cattle at will.' In 1790, when £50 was levied to be laid out in repairs, it was further described as a 'Pack and Prime Way from Kirkby Stephen to Barnard Castle'.[7] As a route to Barnard Castle it has long been abandoned, but its importance lay in the fact that from Raven Seat onwards it led to the coal pits around Tan Hill, a stretch marked as 'jagger road', now also indistinguishable from the moor.

At and near Tan Hill were several pits — Kettlepot, King's Pit, Taylor Rigg and others, not all in Yorkshire, some worked from the thirteenth century. In the seventeenth century, coal for Lady Anne Clifford's castles came from her pits on Stainmore.[8] That for Appleby Castle would be taken via Brough and Warcop, but that for Pendragon would come by Raven Seat. In 1670 when Philip Lord Wharton leased 'Tanhill Pitts' to a partnership for nine years, it was stipulated that his servants were to fetch up to 150 loads a year for the use of Wharton Hall.[9] Carried on packhorses, these too would come by Raven Seat. There is a small packhorse bridge there to this day.

In 1788 one of the deponents at Quarter Sessions was Mary Moore, then aged sixty-six. She said that her father had kept a public house at Raven Seat and that in his time eleven families lived there. Another witness, John Mason of Nateby near Kirkby Stephen, said that he remembered seven families or houses and he had known the road for thirty-five years. He had travelled it with packhorses, and carried meal and potatoes to Raven Seat and brought back coals — a customary two-way traffic. There could well have been a coal depot at Raven Seat. There were then enough people to support a chapel, probably of the Inghamite sect which flourished not far away in Westmorland. The small building they used is much earlier in date than the Inghamites, who were a group breaking away from the Church of England at the same time as the Wesleyans. In the 1920s there was a pulpit in the building, but whether in place or not is not known.

Prosperity dependent on the coal pits was to fade. Coal brought from south Durham undercut in price that from Tan Hill, and although there were four families and twenty-two men, women and children living at Tan Hill in 1851, by the early nineteenth century the houses at Raven Seat had been reduced to the two of the present day. Cleasbys then lived there, and a Daniel Cleasby built the house on the east side in 1830.[10]

Back on the Birkdale road, now high above the beck, we pass Birkdale Cross, another marker on this ancient route sited a little above the road so that it is well seen from a distance. It is a short shaft of millstone grit bulging slightly at the top. Opposite Birkdale Cross on the other side of the beck alongside Great Lodge Gill is Lodge Close, a small green enclosure and a barn, standing out against the sombre moorland as the first sign of cultivation. Up to about thirty years ago, hay was made there for the sheep. Closer to the beck is Horsefolds, a four acre enclosure with an evocative name, now known as Rakestraws after a former owner.

Soon the first habitation appears, Crook Seat, backing directly on to the road. (Modern maps spell it Crook Seal, but old ones give Crook Seat.) Now used as a barn, it was built in four stages: a nucleus twenty-one feet long, with two pairs of small, crude, mullion windows built of millstone grit, similar to those of the chapel building at Raven Seat — the oldest buildings in the area and relics of the first simple stone houses replacing wooden ones. At the west end is an eighteenth-century addition, with a chimney and outshut for a staircase . Barns join up and further extend the whole.

Crook Seat was at one time an inn with a sign which read, so tradition relates, 'Good Ale tomorrow for Nothing'. John Harker, the brother of Simon of Crackpot Hall (see the chapter *Base Metal*), lived here in the 1690s, but it had been abandoned as a dwelling before the middle of the last century. It is remembered that one of the farms at Raven Seat had a pasture at Crook Seat, and that a farm man walked the two miles there and two miles back twice a day via a gill called Punch Bowl to milk the cows there. It is an indication of the availability and cheapness of labour in those days. Also, the pasture in front was, some forty years ago, meadowland cut for hay, again an example of the difference in farming practices when formerly every bit of hay was made, however difficult the terrain, whereas now additional hay is bought in from lowland farms. Another recollection of the inn told us many years ago was that, one night, robbers tried to climb in by taking slates off the roof, but shots were fired at them. Next morning bloody tracks led up the moor and it is said later bones were found.

In this wilderness, poachers were undoubtedly troublesome. On smaller moors, keepers could bush and stake them to prevent the then prevalent use of nets for

Crook Seat, Birkdale, and the road from Swaledale to Cumbria.

poaching grouse. Here watch was kept. On the plateau, Height Howe, just east of Crook Seat, are the ruins of a watching house with remains of a fireplace. (Watcher was the old name for gamekeeper.) A similar small ruin, 14½ feet by 10½ feet, situated at 1,758 feet above sea level on the jagger road from Raven Seat to Tan Hill, is Robert's Seat House. Both watching houses afford extensive views. Tan Hill is clearly visible from 'Robersit' as it is called, and Birkdale Tarn, a narrow slit in the moors, from Height Howe.

In the 1930s we remember being told that a keeper was shot in the legs at 'Robersit'. It was a recollection harking back to the mid-nineteenth century when Cherry Kearton, the watcher, was wounded and vowed revenge. (Cherry Kearton was the great-grandfather of the naturalists Richard and Cherry Kearton.) In those days, leadminers from Weardale, armed with guns and bringing dogs with them, came on marauding raids, and one time Kearton on the look-out, probably from Height Howe, spied the gang making for the night at Crook Seat. Going round the dalehead

Crook Seat, upper Swaledale. Note the extent of the first small house on the right, with tiny mullion windows.

farms he mustered about ten men, and laid siege to the building so that next morning the poachers, finding themselves surrounded by armed men, capitulated.[11]

Three-quarters of a mile farther on, a prominent outcrop of millstone grit above the road has the delightful but baffling name of Lops Wath. Massive boulders have fallen down to be utilised as the walls of a sheepfold.

STONE HOUSE TO HOGGARTHS

In a mile and a quarter we reach the junction of becks which meet to become the Swale. Far below the road and in a sheltered place near the river is Stone House, and almost within sight are three other farmhouses — Ellers, Birkdale and Firs — and on the spit of land formed by the becks' meeting the ruined buildings of Lane (Loanin) End leadmine, once reached by a stone bridge, now gone, across Birkdale Beck. Within a radius of a mile and a half which includes Raven Seat are now four occupied farmhouses, whereas formerly there were at least twenty houses, of which the nucleus near the Swale indicates monastic settlement. In the last century, foundations of one or more houses were levelled for mowing in the fields behind Stone House, and in 1737 in that called Croft was a bakehouse. These small separate buildings containing ovens were common in Elizabethan times when houses were wooden and lacking wall ovens. They obviously survived later in remote parts of the country.[12]

On the other side of the Swale from Stone House in Ash Gill there were a further group of houses: Ash Gill, Stirkholme, Whamp House in the field called Whamp, and possibly a dwelling once destroyed by fire in Burnt House Close. A road, still visible, led from Ash Gill along the hillside to Hoggarths Bridge a mile east. The name, Stirkholme, is forgotten, but from 1589 to 1767 Harkers lived there; first James who died in 1650, then several Simons. The family progressed from husbandmen to yeomen, an example of the prosperity possible in the seventeenth century.[13] We should like to think that one of these was Simon Harker the Quaker, but we cannot be sure. A large millstone grit mortar, with on one side the initials and date S H 1678, now ill-defined, has survived from the Harkers of Stirkholme.

On the track from Raven Seat to Keld were other houses — Close Hills and also Fleets House near Hoggarths — all abandoned. Fleets House was occupied by coalminers in 1779, and has been replaced by a large barn on the site near Whitsundale Beck. Birkdale and Ellers farmhouses, the latter only built in 1863, were left in 1922 and 1946 respectively.

In a field, Little Dales, adjoining Birkdale Beck, next to Brown How and west of Stone House, are foundations said to be those of a chapel. 'Birkdale Chap' is marked on Bowen's map of the North Riding, 1750, and on Thomas Kitchin's map in Burn and Nicholson's *History and Antiquities of Westmorland and Cumberland*, 1777. It would appear that there has been an early chapel in Birkdale, long since abandoned. In a survey of the Archdeaconry of Richmond in 1722, an old chapel in a very ruinous condition is described as being eight miles from Muker. Keld is only three miles and Birkdale six.[14] Conclusive evidence on the origin of Birkdale Chapel is lacking.

The name, Stone House, indicates the presence of a former wooden building on this site by the Swale. It is now a range of two seventeenth-century houses and a barn dated 1827. One house is used partly as outbuildings and the other occupied house is embellished with oak panelling contemporary with the house, dividing the rooms both upstairs and down. Outside on the frontstead, a cobbled yard large enough to contain a posse of horsemen, is a pump which was until recently the chief water supply.

In the early nineteenth century Christopher and Margaret Alderson lived here with their three sons, William, George and Charles, and one daughter, Mary. Tragedy struck the family. In 1818, when he was fifty-four, Christopher was drowned crossing the Swale at night, and William and George were involved in an accident when their trap overturned. William, aged twenty-five, was killed and George

Stone House, upper Swaledale.

sustained permanent injury to his hip. George (1802—76) and Charles (1806—66), bachelors for most of their lives, by their zeal for building and improvement were responsible for change in the neighbourhood.

When he was twenty-one George fathered a son, the child of Mary Scott, house-keeper at Stone House, who it is said refused to marry him. The life of this boy, John Alderson Scott (1823—85), is one of the dales' success stories. First apprenticed to a local mason, he migrated to near London, married a builder's daughter, and made a fortune before he was forty, it is thought in the erection of the Holborn Viaduct. John bought Hoggarths Farm, and that and his father's and uncle's Swaledale prop-erty passed to his son, George. Stone House, Pry House and Hoggarths still belong to his descendants.[15]

Then, unlike the present day, even a small farm usually employed a farm man and a maidservant. At Stone House, George and Charles Alderson had two farm men, two women servants and in 1841 had Christopher Peacock, a mason aged sixty-five, living with them.[16] Also, leadminers are said to have lodged there and, when it is remembered that fifty men were employed at Lane End, this corner of Swaledale must have been a lively place.

Life in this large household resembled that of the Garths at Crackpot, except that the emphasis was on sheep. 'We begin salving today', wrote George on the 9th October 1865, 'so that will keep us throng'. He added: 'I never knew sheep so dear. I sold our draught ewes for a guinea each but Edmund [Clarkson of Pry House] had to wait for his customer and sold his for 22s a price I never knew for blackfaced sheep before.' (George would be flabbergasted at today's prices.)

In 1839 when it was sold by auction, the brothers bought Ash Gill Farm (the others including Stirkholme had vanished), and, pulling down the house, they built the present large, handsome barn. They built the two stone bridges over the Swale between Stone House and Hoggarths. In 1858 they carved out a new farm from

The family at Stone House: (from left to right) Albert, James (Jim) Alderson, Margaret Alderson (seated), Isobel, Jim, Mr Dinsdale, Ella Pontefract.

TO BE SOLD

BY AUCTION,

By Mr. John Terry, Auctioneer,

At the house of MR. THOMAS ALDERSON, Innkeeper, at Cathole,
Near Muker, in Swaledale, in the County of York,

On Saturday the 14th day of September, 1839,

At SIX o'clock in the evening precisely,

And subject to such conditions as will be then produced,

ALL THAT VALUABLE COPYHOLD

ESTATE,

CALLED

ASH GILL,

SITUATE WITHIN THE HAMLET OF KELD, IN SWALEDALE AFORESAID,
AND NOW IN THE OCCUPATION OF MR. JOHN HIRD, AS TENANT;

Consisting of a MESSUAGE or DWELLING-HOUSE, Stable, and other
Conveniences, and the following Closes or Parcels of Meadow and Pasture
LAND, viz.---

	A.	R.	P.
Burnt House Close	10	2	38
Whamp, with a barn thereon, ...	4	1	10
East Close, with a barn thereon, ...	4	2	31
Low Close, with a barn thereon, ...	2	2	19
Little Holme or Long Bottom, with a barn thereon, ...	1	0	16
Intack	3	0	38
Calf Piece	0	0	15

Be the said several quantities more or less; and also 11 Cattle GAITS on
GREAT SLEDDELL contiguous thereto; together with a very valuable right of
Common upon the extensive Moors within the manor of Muker.

The Estate is of Copyhold Tenure held as parcel of the Manor
of Muker by payment of the annual Lord's Rent of 3s. 11d.; and
is free from two thirds of the Tithe arising thereon.

MR. ANTHONY CLARKSON of Smithy-holme, or MR. HENRY CHERRY of
Kisdon, will shew the premises; and any further particulars may be known
at the office of MR. WINN, Solicitor, at Askrigg or at Hawes.

The sale bill when Ash Gill was sold in 1839.

Stone House and other land, and built a farmhouse, Pry House, on the roadside. Like all their undertakings, the workmanship here is excellent. Above a porch, covered by a huge stone slab, is a sundial on a large plaque inscribed with their names and the date.

After Charles's death, George, then aged sixty-four, moved to a part of Pry House, taking with him Ann Coates, their housekeeper for more than thirty years, and in 1871 he married her. Ann died two years before he did.

Almost up to being left in 1964, life at Stone House was carried on in the traditional manner. James Alderson (1878—1951) and his wife, Margaret, brought up three sons and four daughters there. It was the largest farm in Birkdale. They kept three horses, three to five cows, about 500 sheep and five or more sheep dogs. As a young man, one of the sons, Jim, bought a horse for £17 at Cowper Day at Kirkby Stephen, and, bringing her back, wondered whether he had 'done right'. Fanny was very lively but became James Alderson's favourite mount.

Mr Jim Alderson and some of the Coldberghers at Becks Meeting.

Self-sufficiency was the theme — rushes and bracken cut for bedding, large amounts of peat harvested on Ash Gill and carried in peat coups across the river to be stacked in the peat house, part of the big barn. Some coal was fetched from Tan Hill and a little from Kirkby Stephen Station. Cheese and butter were home-made, and two fat pigs annually provided pork, ham and bacon. A rare bacon flake, on which these were dried, hung from the rafters of the kitchen. Havercake was formerly baked on a bakestone and hardened off on a cake stool with oak legs.

The kitchen floor was sanded with broken-down lumps of soft millstone grit fetched from Lops Wath, and sharp sand for sharpening scythes was collected on the shores of Birkdale Tarn. Quilts with interleaved padding were made for bedclothes — each daughter had to have one for when she was twenty-one — and 'stobbed' rugs were homemade for the hearth. Garden flowers were cherished in a narrow bed fenced off by a wall in front of the house. Besides the bacon flake fastened to a beam, a perpetual calendar with sliding lats giving the day of the week must have dated back to the brothers, and in the parlour an alcove once contained a cupboard bed. Here, a handsome organ provided an accompaniment for hymns. It was always customary for relations, friends and buyers of lambs to come and stay at Stone House.

In a home so far from a road, provision for winter was of prime concern. Goods were delivered by horses and carts to the main road, whence they were fetched. In the late autumn an additional 10st bag of flour was bought, a stone of sugar, a 14lb tin of treacle, boxes of long bars of soap, a barrel of apples, a bag of turnips, five or six 8st bags of potatoes stored in barrels and a 28lb bucket of lard. Sometimes a box of kippers — eaten for tea or supper — was bought at Kirkby Stephen.

For all the farms in these high lands, wind and snow are the awesome hazards, and there are many stories of grim experiences. It is noteworthy that when the last tenant of Ellers Farm left, it was said that he had never had a bad winter. Children had to be sturdy and the farmers stalwart. One of the girls at Stone House went to Keld to school with her sister, who was seven when she was five, and stayed with relations there from Monday to Friday. It was a three mile walk. 'We thought nothing of it.'

Another friend of ours remembers when he was seven, coming home from school in a blizzard to Harkers House almost as far as Stone House. His family expected his eldest brother, who was breaking stones on the roadside, to take care of him, but the brother had gone elsewhere. Up to Pry House he had other children for company, but then set off across the pastures alone, and could neither open gates nor climb walls in the blizzard. If the farmer from Pry House had not come to look for him, he would have perished.

The sheep go to the tops even in winter, and if caught in a storm the old ewes remember and make their way down to the foddering place, but not all the hoggs and lambs follow them, so that it is a matter of judgement for the farmer to decide whether to gather in the face of threatening weather. He may go up several times for nothing. Sometimes sheep have to have ice knocked off their fleeces before they can move, and they can be frozen to the ground by their horns or buried in drifts. It is remembered that, years ago, one ewe was missed in a gathering in winter and given up for lost, but next spring she turned up with two lambs at Becks Meetings.

Dogs are of course essential, and especially treasured if they have the nose for setting sheep overblown in drifts. To gather in such places as High Seat, a farmer may take three dogs so as to use them in turn and not tire them out.

Sheep were not always as now the main stock on the farm. There were two cow pastures: Little Moor Pasture, eighty-four acres, was situated north-west of Hoggarths Bridge; and Sleddale Close, 150 acres, was in Great Sleddale. The former was enclosed in 1819 when there were three holders of cattle gates, one the brothers at Stone House, then minors, who were allotted thirty-nine acres.[18] Usually the old cow pastures of the dales villages were situated on hillsides above the meadowland, but Sleddale Close is out of the ordinary. It was on Angram Out Moor and, although situated two and a half miles from that hamlet, Angram farmers owned the cattle gates. Over the years, because of its convenience, Keld and Birkdale farmers bought some cattle gates, for instance chiefly in the seventeenth century the Harkers at Ash Gill bought eleven piecemeal. Sleddale Close was enclosed in the middle of the last century, when walls were built to divide the allotments. Now nine farmers from Angram and Birkdale have land there. There are two barns and meadows where hay was made and stored. Those without barns made stacks. No hay is made there now, but many years ago we have seen people setting off up Great Sleddale on horseback to hay-make — tiny figures disappearing as if to nowhere in the vast landscape.

One day in October about fifty years ago, Mrs John Alderson, then a girl, well remembers going there from Hill Top Farm, one of the farms on a road to Raven Seat with rights in Sleddale. Whilst they were there, it came on to snow. Unprepared and without coats they were perished. 'Father said "Work to keep warm". We sheltered a bit and then went back to Stone House where they were baking. We were given tea and apple pie. I've never tasted anything better before or since.'

Well beyond Sleddale Close, on the east side of the beck, is the shaft of a copper mine worked by a Mr Ward of Reeth in the last century, and on the west side at about 1,800 feet above sea level is a small dam, a hush gutter and a shaft of Leaden Haw leadmine. On the cliff face above the shaft of the copper mine, red campion, lady's mantle and other flowers associated with more lowland habitats bloom in summer (as at Blue John Holes). What difficult places these were to reach, never mind work there! Leaden Haw may well have been worked in the 1750s when leadmining was in progress in Birkdale.[19]

Lane End mine, being so near the river, was unworkable without either or both water wheels and an engine for pumping. In 1801 a partnership of ten, including

Thomas Butson and E A Knowles (see *Base Metal*), took a lease but were drowned out. In this period another of the partners, Richard Garth of Crackpot, carted large quantities of wood, and was working there for weeks on buildings and a wheel case. On the 26th January 1802 he 'went to Bows to see a Water engine about Lonen End'. In 1829 the mine was leased for twenty-one years by Henry Jackson and partners, a group mostly from Kirkby Stephen. The Pomfret/Denys lessors

Hill Top farmhouse, upper Swaledale, with Hill Top Quarry in the foreground. On the far hillside, just above the house, can be seen the walls of Adam Fold, a large old sheepfold now called Addy Fold.

Cooper Metcalfe at Hill Top Quarry, 1948.

stipulated that an engine be installed and fifty men employed.[20] The 80 hp engine took a team of seventeen horses to drag it there, so it is said, and at great expense. Another difficulty was leading coal to the place.

It was for this mine and even more so for Little Moor Foot mine, where there was another engine, a mile down the river, that a complex of water courses were made. One tapped Birkdale Beck below Birkdale farmhouse, passed behind Stone House and followed just above the river to Little Moor Foot. Another, starting at Birkdale

Tarn, fed a small reservoir and thence was piped to the engine of this mine. But the four-mile water race in Birkdale feeding the tarn is by far the most ambitious and remarkable feat. All cut by hand, what work they represented!

An old friend, Cooper Metcalfe (c1876-1947), was born in the house, now ruined, at Lane End, where his father, Thomas Metcalfe, was the engine man. He told us many years ago that about 1850, when his father was about thirty, he lost his right arm in an accident. Jane, his wife, had fashioned a cuff which buttoned across to secure the sleeve, but, when he was reaching out to grease the engine, the sleeve caught higher up. First his hand had to be amputated and then the forearm. Eventually he had a hook fitted.

Cooper was the youngest of a family of ten, and he remembered another near-disaster when one of the boys was almost drowned in the Swale, and was dragged out by his sister. The Metcalfes must have left Lane End when Cooper was an infant.

When the leadmine company, which had also worked Hill Top quarry near Birkdale Tarn, closed down in the 1860s, Thomas took the quarry. Much later three sons were working there, supplying stone chiefly to Kirkby Stephen and Westmorland. In 1925 they fulfilled an order for twelve gateposts, 14 feet long 6 inches wide and 1 foot at the top. Two were a load for a horse and cart. Hill Top stone was used for buildings for miles around, and the warm brown and yellow sandstone of flags and wall tops, scrupulously cleaned, so often seen in Swaledale, is from this well-known quarry.

In his reminiscences Cooper went on to tell us that when he was thirteen he started work at Tan Hill pit. At first he pushed out tubs, then started hewing. On piece-work rates he was paid 6d for filling a tub and 2½d for each tub carried out, usually averaging fifteen to sixteen tubs a day. In the General Strike in 1926 he earned the then large sum of £100 between June and December.

One December day, Cooper, along with two other men, was trapped by a fall of stone for three hours, a not uncommon occurrence. The escape route up a shaft on the north side of the pit required someone to pull them out, and there was no-one there. So they made a little hole through the stones and carefully poked it wider with a length of rail. Whooh! blew the wind. Eventually they squeezed through, and then had to walk up to their thighs in water. 'It was t' worst night as I ivver knawed.' Tan Hill pit closed, and when we knew Cooper he was working Hill Top quarry singlehanded.

The last farmhouse in this survey, Hoggarths, now stands high up in a plantation of trees on the north side of the river and the highway. Formerly it was in Great Ash Gill on the south side of the river, where a barn, a few elms and three lime trees now mark the site. In this cosy nook there were two eighteenth-century houses partly built into the hill, side by side. In front was a grassy paddock, and behind a smaller paddock with a spring.

Hill Top Quarry, upper Swaledale, one of the many small quarries in the Dales where stone and roofing slates were quarried for houses, barns, bridges, paving and walls in the surrounding neighbourhood.

In the late nineteenth century, William and Elizabeth Kilburn and their daughters occupied the top house, the other being used as outbuildings, and their experiences on the 4th July 1899 have been passed down in vivid detail in the family.[21] The day started close and thundery, and they were in two minds whether to gather the sheep for clipping or to fetch coal from Tan Hill. They opted for Tan Hill, and William, returning about noon, tipped out the coal, put up the cart shafts and led the horse still harnessed into the stable, meaning to attend to it after they had had a meal.

It was raining hard by now and water began running into the yard, which was not unusual. Elizabeth took a besom to sweep it out of the front door. William went on eating, declaring that he 'wasn't going to shift for a sup o' watter'. But very soon they saw water rushing down the gill and heard the noise of clashing boulders. The women ran upstairs and, as William came up too, water followed him up step by step until it was door-top height. He put his heavy boot through the landing window and they all escaped on to the hillside. This well-known flood, the result of a

Hoggarths after the cloudburst on the 4th July 1899. The upper house was the one occupied, and the house in the centre was then used as outbuildings.

triple cloudburst on Great Shunnor Fell, did enormous damage to houses, bridges and land here and elsewhere.

When it subsided in Ash Gill, William found the horse standing tied up in its stall, up to its belly in sludge and its head held high. A very good sheepdog chained up in the next stall had slipped its collar and run away to Stone House. A puppy which had been lying in front of the fire in the house was found straddled across a wringing machine. There were two pigs in a sty with half doors opening inwards. They were swimming round and round so exhausted that when the door was opened and the water released, they staggered out and fell down on the ground.

The cart and the coal had disappeared. The front door was taken off its hinges and the house wall damaged. All the paddocks were covered with soil and boulders which took years to clear, and the spring never reappeared. Fortunately the family had Ellers Farm and went to live there. A cup and saucer found intact after the storm at Bridge End a mile down stream is still preserved by a descendant. We have also been told that a lustre jug from the house was found intact at Rowleth Bottom twelve miles down the dale. But perhaps this is apocryphal.

The landlord built a new house, the one we now see on the hill, with stone from the old house and from leadmine buildings. The porch taken from the pumping house of Little Moor Foot mine is an example of the skill of the masons employed there.

Hoggarths Bridge nearby was one of several washed away. An important crossing of the Swale, a temporary bridge had to be put up, and then a substantial stone bridge was erected with the aid of a county grant. It used to be here that farmers' wives took their butter and eggs to sell to Thomas Guy from Muker, who brought potatoes and vegetables, hence its local name — the butter bridge.

A little moral rhyme is associated with Little Moor Foot mine near to Hoggarths Bridge, told us by Cooper Metcalfe. Will Harker, a mine carter who took lead away, used to bring back goods for the miners. Once in a flood he asked their help in carrying lead across the river, and they refused. Later when they sought his help to cross in his cart, he said:

Ill for ill as long as thou will
Good for ill ah nivver will

When we first visited the head of Swaledale in the 1930s, there were twelve occupied farmhouses in the area. Ellers was still occupied. Stone House was left in 1964 and is now worked from Keld. Black How, Hill Top and Harker's House on the road to Raven Seat were left as farmhouses in 1969, 1964 and 1971 respectively. Their land and the sheep, sometimes split up, have been joined up with other farms. Black How is permanently occupied at present, but not as a farmhouse. Most of the houses have been sold off and bought for country cottages.

As late as 1871 there were eighty-five men, women and children in the high dale upwards from Hoggarths. In 1981 there were twenty-four inhabitants in the five occupied farmhouses at Firs, Pry House, Hoggarths and two at Raven Seat, and including the occupants of Black How. Some of the farms were too small to be viable. In the last century Ralph Metcalfe, hind at Ellers, earned 10s a week, a wage which his wife found unacceptable. All the farmhouses are situated at 1,250 to 1,500 feet above sea level, and most off the main road were reached down steep, boggy tracks, difficult enough for horses but treacherous for tractors and impossible for motor vehicles. In 1961 the then very boggy road to Raven Seat from the main road was repaired and laid with tarmac by the county. Also, last but not least, employment in industry ceased.

The communities of Birkdale and Raven Seat are sadly diminished in numbers, and, if it were not for hill-sheep subsidies, the farms would not survive. The nearest village, Keld, has neither school, post office nor a weekly bank which it once had. The remote valleys of the Yorkshire Dales are under threat, and those in authority must be vigilant in the future lest worse befall.

1   *Yorkshire Lay Subsidy* 1301, edited by Wm Brown. Yorks Arch Soc Record Series, vol XXI (1897), p 8.
2   See 'Base Metal', p40.
3   NYCRO PR/MUK/1/1.
4   *Depositions of York Castle*, Surtees Soc, Vol. 40, pp 147-150.
5   *Yorkshire Quarterly Meeting Burials Digest*, 1570-1837, and Richard Robinson, *A Blast Blown out of the North*, 1680, p 23. Information given by Mr D Hall.
6   Parke Account book, 1766-1770. MS now lodged at the North Yorkshire County Record Office.
7   NYCRO QSM 3/2 Northallerton Sessions, 1788, p 106; Thirsk Sessions, 1789; Richmond Sessions, 1790. Supplied by Mr M Y Ashcroft and Mrs A Hill. Also notes made from depositions of witnesses by E R Fawcett.
8   G Williamson, *Lady Anne Clifford*, 1922, pp 510, 512.
9   Lease, Philip Lord Wharton to Christopher Handby and Leonard Wharton for nine years, Tan Hill pits, 1670. Lent by Mr C Clarkson.
10   E. Cooper, *Men of Swaledale*, p 35.
11   Notes made by E R Fawcett.
12   Admittance Muker Manor Court Records. Richard Alderson, two houses etc and Croft with a Bakehouse thereon, 1737. Lent by Mrs J A Nadin and Mrs J Purkes.
13   Indenture 1589, Brian Shawe to James Harkey and admittances to Muker Manor Court. Lent by Mrs J A Nadin and Mrs J Purkes.
14   Leeds Archives Department, RD/RU, Richmond Survey.
15   Family history from Mrs J A Nadin, Mrs J Purkes and Mr R Scott.
16   PRO H0107/46 Muker enumerated census.
17   We are greatly indebted to Mr and Mrs J Alderson, Mr and Mrs C Alderson, Mr and Mrs C Kearton, and Mrs W Raw for recollections of Stone House and general information about Birkdale.
18   Little Moor Pasture Award, 1819. MS lent by Mrs J A Nadin and Mrs J Purkes. The public highway ran through the southern border of the pasture, and one of the stones erected on it inscribed GAC (George and Charles Alderson) is still to be seen on the left hand side of the road above Hoggarths. The three owners of land had to keep up the road and the stone posts marked their allotted lengths.

19   Parke Account Book, 1766--1770.
20   Brotherton Library, Jennings MS, p 257, lease to Thomas Butson and partners 1801;
        NYCRO ZLB/12, Lease, Pomfret/Denys to H Jackson and partners 1829. A heavy brass
        bearing from the engine still exists.
21   Family recollections of the flood from Mr G and Mr W Calvert.

Index